Just The facts101
Textbook Key Facts

Textbook Outlines, Highlights, and Practice Quizzes

Framework for Marketing Management

by Philip Kotler, 6 Edition

All "Just the Facts101" Material Written or Prepared by Cram101 Textbook Reviews

Title Page

WHY STOP HERE... THERE'S MORE ONLINE

With technology and experience, we've developed tools that make studying easier and efficient. Like this Facts101 textbook notebook, **JustTheFacts101.com** offers you the highlights from every chapter of your actual textbook. However, unlike this notebook, **JustTheFacts101.com** gives you practice tests for each of the chapters. You also get access to in-depth reference material for writing essays and papers.

JustTheFacts101.COM FEATURES:

Outlines & Highlights
Just like the ones in this notebook, but with links to additional information.

Integrated Note Taking
Add your class notes to the Facts101 notes, print them and maximize your study time.

Problem Solving
Step-by-step walk throughs for math, stats and other disciplines.

Practice Exams
Five different test taking formats for every chapter.

Easy Access
Study any of your books, on any computer, anywhere.

Unlimited Textbooks
All the features above for virtually all your textbooks, just add them to your account at no additional cost.

By purchasing this book, you get 50% off the normal monthly subscription fee! Just enter the promotional code **'DK73DW28053'** on the Jtf101.com registration screen.

STUDYING MADE EASY

This Facts101 notebook is designed to make studying easier and increase your comprehension of the textbook material. Instead of starting with a blank notebook and trying to write down everything discussed in class lectures, you can use this Facts101 textbook notebook and annotate your notes along with the lecture.

Our goal is to give you the best tools for success.

For a supreme understanding of the course, pair your notebook with our online tools. Should you decide you prefer jtf101.com as your study tool,

we'd like to offer you a trade...

Our Trade In program is a simple way for us to keep our promise and provide you the best studying tools, regardless of where you purchased your Facts101 textbook notebook. As long as your notebook is in *Like New Condition**, you can send it back to us and we will immediately give you a JustTheFacts101.com account free for 120 days!

Let The Trade In Begin!

THREE SIMPLE STEPS TO TRADE:

1. Go to www.jtf101.com/tradein and fill out the packing slip information.
2. Submit and print the packing slip and mail it in with your Facts101 textbook notebook.
3. Activate your account after you receive your email confirmation.

* Books must be returned in *Like New Condition*, meaning there is no damage to the book including, but not limited to; ripped or torn pages, markings or writing on pages, or folded / creased pages. Upon receiving the book, Facts101 will inspect it and reserves the right to terminate your free Facts101.com account and return your textbook notebook at the owners expense.

facts101
LEARNING SYSTEM

"Just the Facts101" is a Content Technologies publication and tool designed to give you all the facts from your textbooks. Visit JustTheFacts101.com for the full practice test for each of your chapters for virtually any of your textbooks.

Facts101 has built custom study tools specific to your textbook. We provide all of the factual testable information and unlike traditional study guides, we will never send you back to your textbook for more information.

YOU WILL NEVER HAVE TO HIGHLIGHT A BOOK AGAIN!

Facts101 StudyGuides
All of the information in this StudyGuide is written specifically for your textbook. We include the key terms, places, people, and concepts... the information you can expect on your next exam!

Want to take a practice test?
Throughout each chapter of this StudyGuide you will find links to JustTheFacts101.com where you can select specific chapters to take a complete test on, or you can subscribe and get practice tests for up to 12 of your textbooks, along with other exclusive Jtf101.com tools like problem solving labs and reference libraries.

JustTheFacts101.com
Only Jtf101.com gives you the outlines, highlights, and PRACTICE TESTS specific to your textbook. JustTheFacts101.com is an online application where you'll discover study tools designed to make the most of your limited study time.

By purchasing this book, you get 50% off the normal monthly subscription fee!. Just enter the promotional code **'DK73DW28053'** on the Jtf101.com registration screen.

www.JustTheFacts101.com

Copyright © 2016 by Content Technologies, Inc. All rights reserved.
"Just the FACTS101"®, "Cram101"® and "Never Highlight a Book Again!"® are registered trademarks of Content Technologies, Inc.
ISBN(s): 9781497062405. PUBI-7.201648

facts101

Framework for Marketing Management
Philip Kotler, 6

CONTENTS

1. Defining Marketing for the New Realities 5
2. Developing and Implementing Marketing Strategies and Plans 17
3. Capturing Marketing Insights and Forecasting Demand 26
4. Creating Long-Term Loyalty Relationships 39
5. Analyzing Consumer and Business Markets 46
6. Identifying Market Segments and Targets 55
7. Crafting the Brand Positioning and Competing Effectively 63
8. Creating Brand Equity and Driving Growth 71
9. Setting Product Strategy and Introducing New Offerings 79
10. Designing and Managing Services 89
11. Developing Pricing Strategies and Programs 98
12. Designing and Managing Integrated Marketing Channels 109
13. Managing Retailing, Wholesaling, and Logistics 121
14. Designing and Managing Integrated Marketing Communications 129
15. Managing Mass Communications: Advertising, Sales Promotions, Events an 139
16. Managing Digital Communications: Online, Social Media, and Mobile 149
17. Managing Personal Communications: Direct and Database Marketing and Pe 157
18. Managing Marketing Responsibly in the Global Economy 166

1. Defining Marketing for the New Realities

CHAPTER OUTLINE: KEY TERMS, PEOPLE, PLACES, CONCEPTS

	Brand
	Life
	Marketing communications
	Brand equity
	Big data
	Chief Information Officer
	Marketing management
	Good
	Marketing
	Services marketing
	Market
	Social marketing
	Demographic
	Need
	Product
	Value proposition
	Demand
	Customer
	Earned media
	Impression
	Media planner

1. Defining Marketing for the New Realities
CHAPTER OUTLINE: KEY TERMS, PEOPLE, PLACES, CONCEPTS

	Supply chain
	Model
	Globalization
	Department store
	Disintermediation
	Consumer-to-consumer
	Product concept
	Selling
	Relationship marketing
	Integrated marketing
	Marketing mix
	Promotion
	Triple bottom line
	Performance
	Plan
	Task

1. Defining Marketing for the New Realities

CHAPTER HIGHLIGHTS & NOTES: KEY TERMS, PEOPLE, PLACES, CONCEPTS

Brand	Brand is the 'name, term, design, symbol, or any other feature that identifies one seller's product distinct from those of other sellers.' Brands are used in business, marketing, and advertising. Initially, livestock branding was adopted to differentiate one person's cattle from another's by means of a distinctive symbol burned into the animal's skin with a hot branding iron. A modern example of a brand is Coca-Cola which belongs to the Coca-Cola Company.
Life	Life is a breakfast cereal formerly made of whole grain oats, but now also containing corn flour, whole wheat flour, and rice flour. It is distributed by the Quaker Oats Company. It was introduced in 1961. The cereal's advertisements currently sport the slogan 'Life is full of surprises'.
Marketing communications	Marketing communications are messages and related media used to communicate with a market. Marketing communications is the 'promotion' part of the 'marketing mix' or the 'four Ps': price, place, promotion, and product. It can also refer to the strategy used by a company or individual to reach their target market through various types of communication.
Brand equity	Brand equity is a phrase used in the marketing industry which describes the value of having a well-known brand name, based on the idea that the owner of a well-known brand name can generate more money from products with that brand name than from products with a less well known name, as consumers believe that a product with a well-known name is better than products with less well-known names. Some marketing researchers have concluded that brands are one of the most valuable assets a company has, as brand equity is one of the factors which can increase the financial value of a brand to the brand owner, although not the only one. Elements that can be included in the valuation of brand equity include (but not limited to): changing market share, profit margins, consumer recognition of logos and other visual elements, brand language associations made by consumers, consumers' perceptions of quality and other relevant brand values.
Big data	Big data is a blanket term for any collection of data sets so large and complex that it becomes difficult to process using on-hand database management tools or traditional data processing applications. The challenges include capture, curation, storage, search, sharing, transfer, analysis and visualization. The trend to larger data sets is due to the additional information derivable from analysis of a single large set of related data, as compared to separate smaller sets with the same total amount of data, allowing correlations to be found to 'spot business trends, determine quality of research, prevent diseases, link legal citations, combat crime, and determine real-time roadway traffic conditions.'

1. Defining Marketing for the New Realities

CHAPTER HIGHLIGHTS & NOTES: KEY TERMS, PEOPLE, PLACES, CONCEPTS

Chief Information Officer	Chief Information Officer or Information Technology (IT) Director, is a job title commonly given to the most senior executive in an enterprise responsible for the information technology and computer systems that support enterprise goals. Generally, the Chief Information Officer reports to the chief executive officer, chief operating officer or chief financial officer. In military organizations, they report to the commanding officer.
Marketing management	Marketing management is a business discipline which focuses on the practical application of marketing techniques and the management of a firm's marketing resources and activities. Globalization has led firms to market beyond the borders of their home countries, making international marketing highly significant and an integral part of a firm's marketing strategy. Marketing managers are often responsible for influencing the level, timing, and composition of customer demand accepted definition of the term.
Good	In economics, a good is a material that satisfies human wants and provides utility, for example, to a consumer making a purchase. A common distinction is made between 'goods' that are tangible property (also called goods) and services, which are non-physical. Commodities may be used as a synonym for economic goods but often refer to marketable raw materials and primary products.
Marketing	Marketing is the process of communicating the value of a product or service to customers, for the purpose of selling that product or service. Marketing can be looked at as an organizational function and a set of processes for creating, delivering and communicating value to customers, and customer relationship management that also benefits the organization. Marketing is the science of choosing target markets through market analysis and market segmentation, as well as understanding consumer behavior and providing superior customer value.
Services marketing	Services marketing is a sub field of marketing which covers the marketing of both goods and services. Goods marketing includes the marketing of fast moving consumer goods (FMCG) and durables. Services marketing typically refers to the marketing of both business to consumer (B2C) and business to business (B2B) services.
Market	A market is one of the many varieties of systems, institutions, procedures, social relations and infrastructures whereby parties engage in exchange. While parties may exchange goods and services by barter, most markets rely on sellers offering their goods or services (including labor) in exchange for money from buyers. It can be said that a market is the process by which the prices of goods and services are established.
Social marketing	Social marketing seeks to develop and integrate marketing concepts with other approaches to influence behaviors that benefit individuals and communities for the greater social good.

1. Defining Marketing for the New Realities

CHAPTER HIGHLIGHTS & NOTES: KEY TERMS, PEOPLE, PLACES, CONCEPTS

	It seeks to integrate research, best practice, theory, audience and partnership insight, to inform the delivery of competition sensitive and segmented social change programs that are effective, efficient, equitable and sustainable.
	Although 'social marketing' is sometimes seen only as using standard commercial marketing practices to achieve non-commercial goals, this is an oversimplification.
Demographic	Demographics are the quantifiable statistics of a given population. Demographics are also used to identify the study of quantifiable subsets within a given population which characterize that population at a specific point in time.
	Demography is used widely in public opinion polling and marketing.
Need	A need is something that is necessary for organisms to live a healthy life. Needs are distinguished from wants because a deficiency would cause a clear negative outcome, such as dysfunction or death. Needs can be objective and physical, such as food, or they can be subjective and psychological, such as the need for self-esteem.
Product	In marketing, a product is anything that can be offered to a market that might satisfy a want or need. In retailing, products are called merchandise. In manufacturing, products are bought as raw materials and sold as finished goods.
Value proposition	A value proposition is a promise of value to be delivered and acknowledged and a belief from the customer that value will be delivered and experienced. A value proposition can apply to an entire organization, or parts thereof, or customer accounts, or products or services.
	Creating a value proposition is a part of business strategy.
Demand	In economics, demand is the utility for a good or service of an economic agent, relative to a budget constraint. (Note: This distinguishes 'demand' from 'quantity demanded', where demand is a listing or graphing of quantity demanded at each possible price. In contrast to demand, quantity demanded is the exact quantity demanded at a certain price.
Customer	A customer is the recipient of a good, service, product, or idea, obtained from a seller, vendor, or supplier for a monetary or other valuable consideration. Customers are generally categorized into two types:•An intermediate customer or trade customer who is a dealer that purchases goods for re-sale.•An ultimate customer who does not in turn re-sell the things bought but either passes them to the consumer or actually is the consumer.
	A customer may or may not also be a consumer, but the two notions are distinct, even though the terms are commonly confused. A customer purchases goods; a consumer uses them.

1. Defining Marketing for the New Realities

CHAPTER HIGHLIGHTS & NOTES: KEY TERMS, PEOPLE, PLACES, CONCEPTS

Earned media	Earned media refers to publicity gained through promotional efforts other than advertising, as opposed to paid media, which refers to publicity gained through advertising.
Impression	An impression is a measure of the number of times an ad is seen. Clicking or not is not taken into account. Each time an ad displays it is counted as one impression.
Media planner	Media planning is generally the task of a media agency and entails finding media platforms for a client's brand or product to use. The job of media planning is to determine the best combination of media to achieve the marketing campaign objectives. In the process of planning, the media planner needs to answer questions such as:•How many of the audience can be reached through the various media?•On which media (and ad vehicles) should the ads be placed?•How frequent should the ads be placed?•How much money should be spent in each medium? Choosing which media or type of advertising to use is sometimes tricky for small firms with limited budgets and know-how.
Supply chain	A supply chain is a system of organizations, people, activities, information, and resources involved in moving a product or service from supplier to customer. Supply chain activities transform natural resources, raw materials, and components into a finished product that is delivered to the end customer. In sophisticated supply chain systems, used products may re-enter the supply chain at any point where residual value is recyclable.
Model	A model, is a person in a role either to promote, display, or advertise commercial products (notably fashion clothing) or to serve as a visual aide for people who are creating works of art. Modelling ('modeling' in American English) is considered to be different from other types of public performance, such as an acting, dancing or being a mime artist. The boundary between modelling and performing is, however, not well defined, although such activities as appearing in a movie or a play are almost never labelled as modelling.
Globalization	Globalization is the process of international integration arising from the interchange of world views, products, ideas, and other aspects of culture. Advances in transportation and telecommunications infrastructure, including the rise of the telegraph and its posterity the Internet, are major factors in globalization, generating further interdependence of economic and cultural activities. Though scholars place the origins of globalization in modern times, others trace its history long before the European age of discovery and voyages to the New World.
Department store	A department store is a retail establishment with a building open to the public, offering a wide range of consumer goods.

1. Defining Marketing for the New Realities

CHAPTER HIGHLIGHTS & NOTES: KEY TERMS, PEOPLE, PLACES, CONCEPTS

	It typically allows shoppers to choose between multiple merchandise lines, at variable price points, in different product categories known as 'departments'.
	Department stores usually sell a variety of products, including clothing, furniture, home appliances, toys, cosmetics, gardening, toiletries, sporting goods, do it yourself, paint, and hardware and additionally select other lines of products such as food, books, jewelry, electronics, stationery, photographic equipment, baby needs, and pet supplies.
Disintermediation	In economics, disintermediation is the removal of intermediaries in a supply chain, or 'cutting out the middlemen'. Instead of going through traditional distribution channels, which had some type of intermediate (such as a distributor, wholesaler, broker, or agent), companies may now deal with every customer directly, for example via the Internet. One important factor is a drop in the cost of servicing customers directly.
Consumer-to-consumer	Consumer-to-consumer electronic commerce involves the electronically facilitated transactions between consumers through some third party. A common example is the online auction, in which a consumer posts an item for sale and other consumers bid to purchase it; the third party generally charges a flat fee or commission. The sites are only intermediaries, just there to match consumers.
Product concept	Product concept is the understanding of the dynamics of the product in order to showcase the best qualities and maximum features of the product. Marketers spend a lot of time and research in order to target their attended audience. Marketers will look into a product concept before marketing a product towards their customers.
Selling	Selling is offering to exchange an item of value for a different item. The original item of value being offered may be either tangible or intangible. The second item, usually money, is most often seen by the seller as being of equal or greater value than that being offered for sale.
Relationship marketing	Relationship marketing was first defined as a form of marketing developed from direct response marketing campaigns which emphasizes customer retention and satisfaction, rather than a dominant focus on sales transactions.
	As a practice, relationship marketing differs from other forms of marketing in that it recognizes the long term value of customer relationships and extends communication beyond intrusive advertising and sales promotional messages.
	With the growth of the internet and mobile platforms, relationship marketing has continued to evolve and move forward as technology opens more collaborative and social communication channels.

1. Defining Marketing for the New Realities

CHAPTER HIGHLIGHTS & NOTES: KEY TERMS, PEOPLE, PLACES, CONCEPTS

Integrated marketing	Integrated Marketing Communication is the application of consistent brand messaging across both traditional and non-traditional marketing channels and using different promotional methods to reinforce each other.
Marketing mix	The marketing mix is a business tool used in marketing and by marketers. The marketing mix is often crucial when determining a product or brand's offer, and is often associated with the four P's: price, product, promotion, and place. In service marketing, however, the four Ps are expanded to the seven P's or eight P's to address the different nature of services.
Promotion	Promotion is one of the market mix elements or features, and a term used frequently in marketing. The marketing mix includes the four P's: price, product, promotion, and place. Promotion refers to raising customer awareness of a product or brand, generating sales, and creating brand loyalty.
Triple bottom line	Triple bottom line is an accounting framework with three parts: social, environmental (or ecological) and financial. These three divisions are also called the three Ps: people, planet and profit, or the 'three pillars of sustainability'. Interest in triple bottom line accounting has been growing in both for-profit, nonprofit and government sectors.
Performance	A performance, in performing arts, generally comprises an event in which a performer or group of performers behave in a particular way for another group of people, the audience. Choral music and ballet are examples. Usually the performers participate in rehearsals beforehand.
Plan	A plan is typically any diagram or list of steps with timing and resources, used to achieve an objective. See also strategy. It is commonly understood as a temporal set of intended actions through which one expects to achieve a goal.
Task	In project management, a task is an activity that needs to be accomplished within a defined period of time or by a deadline to work towards work-related goals. A task can be broken down into assignments which should also have a defined start and end date or a deadline for completion. One or more assignments on a task puts the task under execution.

1. Defining Marketing for the New Realities

CHAPTER QUIZ: KEY TERMS, PEOPLE, PLACES, CONCEPTS

1. _____ is the 'name, term, design, symbol, or any other feature that identifies one seller's product distinct from those of other sellers.' _____s are used in business, marketing, and advertising. Initially, livestock branding was adopted to differentiate one person's cattle from another's by means of a distinctive symbol burned into the animal's skin with a hot branding iron. A modern example of a _____ is Coca-Cola which belongs to the Coca-Cola Company.

    a. Back to school
    b. Backward invention
    c. Bass diffusion model
    d. Brand

2. Media planning is generally the task of a media agency and entails finding media platforms for a client's brand or product to use. The job of media planning is to determine the best combination of media to achieve the marketing campaign objectives.

    In the process of planning, the _____ needs to answer questions such as:•How many of the audience can be reached through the various media?•On which media (and ad vehicles) should the ads be placed?•How frequent should the ads be placed?•How much money should be spent in each medium?

    Choosing which media or type of advertising to use is sometimes tricky for small firms with limited budgets and know-how.

    a. Tulip mania
    b. Content farm
    c. Corporate blog
    d. Media planner

3. _____ is a breakfast cereal formerly made of whole grain oats, but now also containing corn flour, whole wheat flour, and rice flour. It is distributed by the Quaker Oats Company. It was introduced in 1961. The cereal's advertisements currently sport the slogan '_____ is full of surprises'.

    a. Bet on Black
    b. Blipvert
    c. Life
    d. Cake

4. A _____ is one of the many varieties of systems, institutions, procedures, social relations and infrastructures whereby parties engage in exchange. While parties may exchange goods and services by barter, most _____s rely on sellers offering their goods or services (including labor) in exchange for money from buyers. It can be said that a _____ is the process by which the prices of goods and services are established.

    a. Total Immersion
    b. Barker channel
    c. Market
    d. Bespoke Music

1. Defining Marketing for the New Realities

CHAPTER QUIZ: KEY TERMS, PEOPLE, PLACES, CONCEPTS

5. A _____ is a system of organizations, people, activities, information, and resources involved in moving a product or service from supplier to customer. _____ activities transform natural resources, raw materials, and components into a finished product that is delivered to the end customer. In sophisticated _____ systems, used products may re-enter the _____ at any point where residual value is recyclable.

   a. 350 West Mart Center
   b. Balance of contract
   c. Supply chain
   d. Bullwhip effect

ANSWER KEY
1. Defining Marketing for the New Realities

1. d
2. d
3. c
4. c
5. c

You can take the complete Chapter Practice Test

for 1. Defining Marketing for the New Realities
on all key terms, persons, places, and concepts.

Online 99 Cents

http://www.JustTheFacts101.com

Use www.JustTheFacts101.com for all your study needs including Facts101's online interactive problem solving labs in chemistry, statistics, mathematics, and more.

2. Developing and Implementing Marketing Strategies and Plans

CHAPTER OUTLINE: KEY TERMS, PEOPLE, PLACES, CONCEPTS

- Strategy
- Benchmarking
- Customer
- Market segmentation
- Service
- Value chain
- Customer relationship management
- Marketing myopia
- Strategic planning
- Supply chain
- Cost
- Management process
- Mission statement
- Shareholder value
- Grid
- Big data
- Goal
- Marketing
- Marketing dashboard
- Customer-perceived value
- Marketing communications

2. Developing and Implementing Marketing Strategies and Plans

CHAPTER OUTLINE: KEY TERMS, PEOPLE, PLACES, CONCEPTS

	Strategic control
	Brand equity

CHAPTER HIGHLIGHTS & NOTES: KEY TERMS, PEOPLE, PLACES, CONCEPTS

Strategy	Strategy is a high level plan to achieve one or more goals under conditions of uncertainty. Strategy is important because the resources available to achieve these goals are usually limited. Strategy generally involves setting goals, determining actions to achieve the goals, and mobilizing resources to execute the actions.
Benchmarking	Benchmarking is the process of comparing one's business processes and performance metrics to industry bests or best practices from other companies. Dimensions typically measured are quality, time and cost. In the process of best practice benchmarking, management identifies the best firms in their industry, or in another industry where similar processes exist, and compares the results and processes of those studied (the 'targets') to one's own results and processes.
Customer	A customer is the recipient of a good, service, product, or idea, obtained from a seller, vendor, or supplier for a monetary or other valuable consideration. Customers are generally categorized into two types:•An intermediate customer or trade customer who is a dealer that purchases goods for re-sale.•An ultimate customer who does not in turn re-sell the things bought but either passes them to the consumer or actually is the consumer. A customer may or may not also be a consumer, but the two notions are distinct, even though the terms are commonly confused. A customer purchases goods; a consumer uses them.
Market segmentation	Market segmentation is a marketing strategy that involves dividing a broad target market into subsets of consumers who have common needs and priorities, and then designing and implementing strategies to target them. Market segmentation strategies may be used to identify the target customers, and provide supporting data for positioning to achieve a marketing plan objective. Businesses may develop product differentiation strategies, or an undifferentiated approach, involving specific products or product lines depending on the specific demand and attributes of the target segment.
Service	In economics, a service is an intangible commodity. That is, services are an example of intangible economic goods.

2. Developing and Implementing Marketing Strategies and Plans

CHAPTER HIGHLIGHTS & NOTES: KEY TERMS, PEOPLE, PLACES, CONCEPTS

Value chain	A value chain is a chain of activities that a firm operating in a specific industry performs in order to deliver a valuable product or service for the market. The concept comes from business management and was first described and popularized by Michael Porter in his 1985 best-seller, Competitive Advantage: Creating and Sustaining Superior Performance. The idea of the value chain is based on the process view of organizations, the idea of seeing a manufacturing (or service) organization as a system, made up of subsystems each with inputs, transformation processes and outputs.
Customer relationship management	Customer relationship management is a system for managing a company's interactions with current and future customers. It involves using technology to organize, automate and synchronize sales, marketing, customer service, and technical support.
Marketing myopia	Marketing myopia is a term used in marketing as well as the title of an important marketing paper written by Theodore Levitt. This paper was first published in 1960 in the Harvard Business Review, a journal of which he was an editor. Marketing Myopia suggests that businesses will do better in the end if they concentrate on meeting customers' needs rather than on selling products.
Strategic planning	Strategic planning is an organization's process of defining its strategy, or direction, and making decisions on allocating its resources to pursue this strategy. It may also extend to control mechanisms for guiding the implementation of the strategy. Strategic planning became prominent in corporations during the 1960s and remains an important aspect of strategic management.
Supply chain	A supply chain is a system of organizations, people, activities, information, and resources involved in moving a product or service from supplier to customer. Supply chain activities transform natural resources, raw materials, and components into a finished product that is delivered to the end customer. In sophisticated supply chain systems, used products may re-enter the supply chain at any point where residual value is recyclable.
Cost	In production, research, retail, and accounting, a cost is the value of money that has been used up to produce something, and hence is not available for use anymore. In business, the cost may be one of acquisition, in which case the amount of money expended to acquire it is counted as cost. In this case, money is the input that is gone in order to acquire the thing.
Management process	Management process is a process of planning and controlling the organizing and leading execution of any type of activity, such as: The organization's senior management is responsible for carrying out its management process. However, this is not always the case for all management processes, for example, it is the responsibility of the project manager to carry out a project management process. •project management•project planning.

2. Developing and Implementing Marketing Strategies and Plans

CHAPTER HIGHLIGHTS & NOTES: KEY TERMS, PEOPLE, PLACES, CONCEPTS

Mission statement	A mission statement is a statement of the purpose of a company, organization or person, its reason for existing. The mission statement should guide the actions of the organization, spell out its overall goal, provide a path, and guide decision-making. It provides 'the framework or context within which the company's strategies are formulated.' It's like a goal for what the company wants to do for the world.
Shareholder value	Shareholder value is a business term, sometimes phrased as shareholder value maximization or as the shareholder value model, which implies that the ultimate measure of a company's success is the extent to which it enriches shareholders. It became popular during the 1980s, and is particularly associated with former CEO of General Electric, Jack Welch. The term used in several ways:•To refer to the market capitalization of a company (rarely used)•To refer to the concept that the primary goal for a company is to increase the wealth of its shareholders (owners) by paying dividends and/or causing the stock price to increase•To refer to the more specific concept that planned actions by management and the returns to shareholders should outperform certain bench-marks such as the cost of capital concept.
Grid	In graphic design, a grid is a structure made up of a series of intersecting straight (vertical, horizontal, and angular) or curved guide lines used to structure content. The grid serves as an armature on which a designer can organize graphic elements (images, glyphs, paragraphs) in a rational, easy to absorb manner. A grid can be use to organize graphic elements in relation to a page, in relation to other graphic elements on the page, or relation to other parts of the same graphic element or shape.
Big data	Big data is a blanket term for any collection of data sets so large and complex that it becomes difficult to process using on-hand database management tools or traditional data processing applications. The challenges include capture, curation, storage, search, sharing, transfer, analysis and visualization. The trend to larger data sets is due to the additional information derivable from analysis of a single large set of related data, as compared to separate smaller sets with the same total amount of data, allowing correlations to be found to 'spot business trends, determine quality of research, prevent diseases, link legal citations, combat crime, and determine real-time roadway traffic conditions.' Scientists regularly encounter limitations due to large data sets in many areas, including meteorology, genomics, connectomics, complex physics simulations, and biological and environmental research.

2. Developing and Implementing Marketing Strategies and Plans

CHAPTER HIGHLIGHTS & NOTES: KEY TERMS, PEOPLE, PLACES, CONCEPTS

Goal	A goal is a desired result a person or a system envisions, plans and commits to achieve a personal or organizational desired end-point in some sort of assumed development. Many people endeavor to reach goals within a finite time by setting deadlines.
	It is roughly similar to purpose or aim, the anticipated result which guides reaction, or an end, which is an object, either a physical object or an abstract object, that has intrinsic value.
Marketing	Marketing is the process of communicating the value of a product or service to customers, for the purpose of selling that product or service.
	Marketing can be looked at as an organizational function and a set of processes for creating, delivering and communicating value to customers, and customer relationship management that also benefits the organization. Marketing is the science of choosing target markets through market analysis and market segmentation, as well as understanding consumer behavior and providing superior customer value.
Marketing dashboard	Marketing performance measurement and management is a term used by marketing professionals to describe the analysis and improvement of the efficiency and effectiveness of marketing. This is accomplished by focus on the alignment of marketing activities, strategies, and metrics with business goals. It involves the creation of a metrics framework to monitor marketing performance, and then develop and utilize marketing dashboards to manage marketing performance.
Customer-perceived value	Value in marketing, also known as customer-perceived value, is the difference between a prospective customer's evaluation of the benefits and costs of one product when compared with others. Value may also be expressed as a straightforward relationship between perceived benefits and perceived costs: Value = Benefits / Cost.
	The customers get benefits and assume costs.
Marketing communications	Marketing communications are messages and related media used to communicate with a market. Marketing communications is the 'promotion' part of the 'marketing mix' or the 'four Ps': price, place, promotion, and product. It can also refer to the strategy used by a company or individual to reach their target market through various types of communication.
Strategic control	Strategic control is a term used to describe the process used by organisations to control the formation and execution of strategic plans; it is a specialised form of management control, and differs from other forms of management control in respects of its need to handle uncertainty and ambiguity at various points in the control process.
	Strategic control is also focused on **the achievement of future goals**, rather than the evaluation of past performance. Vis:

2. Developing and Implementing Marketing Strategies and Plans

CHAPTER HIGHLIGHTS & NOTES: KEY TERMS, PEOPLE, PLACES, CONCEPTS

Brand equity	Brand equity is a phrase used in the marketing industry which describes the value of having a well-known brand name, based on the idea that the owner of a well-known brand name can generate more money from products with that brand name than from products with a less well known name, as consumers believe that a product with a well-known name is better than products with less well-known names. Some marketing researchers have concluded that brands are one of the most valuable assets a company has, as brand equity is one of the factors which can increase the financial value of a brand to the brand owner, although not the only one. Elements that can be included in the valuation of brand equity include (but not limited to): changing market share, profit margins, consumer recognition of logos and other visual elements, brand language associations made by consumers, consumers' perceptions of quality and other relevant brand values.

CHAPTER QUIZ: KEY TERMS, PEOPLE, PLACES, CONCEPTS

1. _____ is a phrase used in the marketing industry which describes the value of having a well-known brand name, based on the idea that the owner of a well-known brand name can generate more money from products with that brand name than from products with a less well known name, as consumers believe that a product with a well-known name is better than products with less well-known names.

   Some marketing researchers have concluded that brands are one of the most valuable assets a company has, as _____ is one of the factors which can increase the financial value of a brand to the brand owner, although not the only one. Elements that can be included in the valuation of _____ include (but not limited to): changing market share, profit margins, consumer recognition of logos and other visual elements, brand language associations made by consumers, consumers' perceptions of quality and other relevant brand values.

   a. Product management
   b. Brand equity
   c. Big Data Partnership
   d. CloverETL

2. . Value in marketing, also known as _____, is the difference between a prospective customer's evaluation of the benefits and costs of one product when compared with others. Value may also be expressed as a straightforward relationship between perceived benefits and perceived costs: Value = Benefits / Cost.

   The customers get benefits and assume costs.

   a. Servicescape
   b. reverse marketing

2. Developing and Implementing Marketing Strategies and Plans

CHAPTER QUIZ: KEY TERMS, PEOPLE, PLACES, CONCEPTS

   c. Tulip mania
   d. Customer-perceived value

3. _____ is a high level plan to achieve one or more goals under conditions of uncertainty. _____ is important because the resources available to achieve these goals are usually limited.

   _____ generally involves setting goals, determining actions to achieve the goals, and mobilizing resources to execute the actions.

   a. BLUF
   b. Choice
   c. Commercial area
   d. Strategy

4. A _____ is a chain of activities that a firm operating in a specific industry performs in order to deliver a valuable product or service for the market. The concept comes from business management and was first described and popularized by Michael Porter in his 1985 best-seller, Competitive Advantage: Creating and Sustaining Superior Performance. '

   The idea of the _____ is based on the process view of organizations, the idea of seeing a manufacturing (or service) organization as a system, made up of subsystems each with inputs, transformation processes and outputs.'

   a. Tulip mania
   b. Cargo
   c. Case
   d. Value chain

5. _____ is the process of comparing one's business processes and performance metrics to industry bests or best practices from other companies. Dimensions typically measured are quality, time and cost. In the process of best practice _____, management identifies the best firms in their industry, or in another industry where similar processes exist, and compares the results and processes of those studied (the 'targets') to one's own results and processes.

   a. complexity management
   b. First-mover advantage
   c. First-mover
   d. Benchmarking

**ANSWER KEY
2. Developing and Implementing Marketing Strategies and Plans**

1. b
2. d
3. d
4. d
5. d

You can take the complete Chapter Practice Test

for 2. Developing and Implementing Marketing Strategies and Plans
on all key terms, persons, places, and concepts.

Online 99 Cents

http://www.JustTheFacts101.com

Use www.JustTheFacts101.com for all your study needs

including Facts101's online interactive problem solving labs in

chemistry, statistics, mathematics, and more.

3. Capturing Marketing Insights and Forecasting Demand

CHAPTER OUTLINE: KEY TERMS, PEOPLE, PLACES, CONCEPTS

- _____ Behavioral targeting
- _____ Big data
- _____ Data mining
- _____ Data warehouse
- _____ Database marketing
- _____ Marketing information system
- _____ Marketing management
- _____ Advertising
- _____ Marketing
- _____ Marketing intelligence
- _____ Marketing research
- _____ Mission statement
- _____ Social marketing
- _____ Social media
- _____ Focus group
- _____ Industry classification
- _____ Observational research
- _____ Primary data
- _____ Secondary data
- _____ Survey research
- _____ Galvanometer

3. Capturing Marketing Insights and Forecasting Demand

CHAPTER OUTLINE: KEY TERMS, PEOPLE, PLACES, CONCEPTS

_____ QR code

_____ Questionnaire

_____ Tachistoscope

_____ Data collection

_____ Forecasting

_____ Sales

_____ Market share

_____ Gross domestic product

_____ Demographic

_____ Diversity

_____ Consumer

_____ Social network

_____ View

_____ Innovation

_____ Market testing

3. Capturing Marketing Insights and Forecasting Demand

CHAPTER HIGHLIGHTS & NOTES: KEY TERMS, PEOPLE, PLACES, CONCEPTS

Behavioral targeting	Behavioral targeting refers to a range of technologies and techniques used by online website publishers and advertisers aimed at increasing the effectiveness of advertising using user web-browsing behavior information. In particular, 'behavioral targeting uses information collected from an individual's web-browsing behavior (e.g., the pages that they have visited or the searches they have conducted) to select advertisements to display'. When a consumer visits a web site, the pages they visit, the amount of time they view each page, the links they click on, the searches they make and the things that they interact with, allow sites to collect that data, and other factors, create a 'profile' that links to that visitor's web browser.
Big data	Big data is a blanket term for any collection of data sets so large and complex that it becomes difficult to process using on-hand database management tools or traditional data processing applications. The challenges include capture, curation, storage, search, sharing, transfer, analysis and visualization. The trend to larger data sets is due to the additional information derivable from analysis of a single large set of related data, as compared to separate smaller sets with the same total amount of data, allowing correlations to be found to 'spot business trends, determine quality of research, prevent diseases, link legal citations, combat crime, and determine real-time roadway traffic conditions.' Scientists regularly encounter limitations due to large data sets in many areas, including meteorology, genomics, connectomics, complex physics simulations, and biological and environmental research.
Data mining	Data mining, an interdisciplinary subfield of computer science, is the computational process of discovering patterns in large data sets involving methods at the intersection of artificial intelligence, machine learning, statistics, and database systems. The overall goal of the data mining process is to extract information from a data set and transform it into an understandable structure for further use. Aside from the raw analysis step, it involves database and data management aspects, data pre-processing, model and inference considerations, interestingness metrics, complexity considerations, post-processing of discovered structures, visualization, and online updating.
Data warehouse	In computing, a data warehouse, or an enterprise data warehouse is a system used for reporting and data analysis. Integrating data from one or more disparate sources creates a central repository of data, a data warehouse. Data warehouses store current and historical data and are used for creating trending reports for senior management reporting such as annual and quarterly comparisons.
Database marketing	Database marketing is a form of direct marketing using databases of customers or potential customers to generate personalized communications in order to promote a product or service for marketing purposes.

3. Capturing Marketing Insights and Forecasting Demand

CHAPTER HIGHLIGHTS & NOTES: KEY TERMS, PEOPLE, PLACES, CONCEPTS

	The method of communication can be any addressable medium, as in direct marketing.
	The distinction between direct and database marketing stems primarily from the attention paid to the analysis of data.
Marketing information system	A marketing information system is a management information system designed to support marketing decision making. Jobber (2007) defines it as a 'system in which marketing data is formally gathered, stored, analysed and distributed to managers in accordance with their informational needs on a regular basis.' In addition, the online business dictionary defines Marketing Information System as "a system that analyzes and assesses marketing information, gathered continuously from sources inside and outside an organization." Furthermore, "an overall Marketing Information System can be defined as a set structure of procedures and methods for the regular, planned collection, analysis and presentation of information for use in making marketing decisions." (Kotler, at al, 2006) Developing a MkIS system is becoming extremely important as the strength of economies rely on services and to better understand the specific needs of customers. Kotler, et al. (2006) defined it more broadly as 'people, equipment, and procedures to gather, sort, analyze, evaluate, and distribute needed, timely, and accurate information to marketing decision makers.' As our economy focuses on services, marketing is becoming extremely important to "monitor the marketing environment for changes in buyer behavior competition, technology, economic conditions, and government policies." In this sense, the role of marketing is becoming pivotal for an organization to "adapt to changes in the market environment." (Harmon, 2003) Furthermore, as our economy relies heavily on the acquisition of knowledge, MkIS systems are necessary to be able to define and differentiate the value proposition that one organization provides with respect to another, as well as to define their competitive advantage.
Marketing management	Marketing management is a business discipline which focuses on the practical application of marketing techniques and the management of a firm's marketing resources and activities. Globalization has led firms to market beyond the borders of their home countries, making international marketing highly significant and an integral part of a firm's marketing strategy. Marketing managers are often responsible for influencing the level, timing, and composition of customer demand accepted definition of the term.
Advertising	Advertising or advertizing in business is a form of marketing communication used to encourage, persuade, or manipulate an audience to take or continue to take some action. Most commonly, the desired result is to drive consumer behavior with respect to a commercial offering, although political and ideological advertising is also common. This type of work belongs to a category called affective labor.

3. Capturing Marketing Insights and Forecasting Demand

CHAPTER HIGHLIGHTS & NOTES: KEY TERMS, PEOPLE, PLACES, CONCEPTS

Marketing	Marketing is the process of communicating the value of a product or service to customers, for the purpose of selling that product or service.
	Marketing can be looked at as an organizational function and a set of processes for creating, delivering and communicating value to customers, and customer relationship management that also benefits the organization. Marketing is the science of choosing target markets through market analysis and market segmentation, as well as understanding consumer behavior and providing superior customer value.
Marketing intelligence	Marketing intelligence is the everyday information relevant to a company's markets, gathered and analyzed specifically for the purpose of accurate and confident decision-making in determining market opportunity, market penetration strategy, and market development metrics. Marketing intelligence is necessary when entering a foreign market.
	Marketing intelligence determines the intelligence needed, collects it by searching environment and delivers it to marketing managers who need it.
Marketing research	Marketing research is 'the process or set of processes that links the consumers, customers, and end users to the marketer through information -- information used to identify and define marketing opportunities and problems; generate, refine, and evaluate marketing actions; monitor marketing performance; and improve understanding of marketing as a process. Marketing research specifies the information required to address these issues, designs the method for collecting information, manages and implements the data collection process, analyzes the results, and communicates the findings and their implications.'
	It is the systematic gathering, recording, and analysis of qualitative and quantitative data about issues relating to marketing products and services. The goal of marketing research is to identify and assess how changing elements of the marketing mix impacts customer behavior.
Mission statement	A mission statement is a statement of the purpose of a company, organization or person, its reason for existing.
	The mission statement should guide the actions of the organization, spell out its overall goal, provide a path, and guide decision-making. It provides 'the framework or context within which the company's strategies are formulated.' It's like a goal for what the company wants to do for the world.
Social marketing	Social marketing seeks to develop and integrate marketing concepts with other approaches to influence behaviors that benefit individuals and communities for the greater social good. It seeks to integrate research, best practice, theory, audience and partnership insight, to inform the delivery of competition sensitive and segmented social change programs that are effective, efficient, equitable and sustainable.

3. Capturing Marketing Insights and Forecasting Demand

CHAPTER HIGHLIGHTS & NOTES: KEY TERMS, PEOPLE, PLACES, CONCEPTS

Social media	Social media is the social interaction among people in which they create, share or exchange information and ideas in virtual communities and networks. Andreas Kaplan and Michael Haenlein define social media as 'a group of Internet-based applications that build on the ideological and technological foundations of Web 2.0, and that allow the creation and exchange of user-generated content.' Furthermore, social media depend on mobile and web-based technologies to create highly interactive platforms through which individuals and communities share, co-create, discuss, and modify user-generated content. They introduce substantial and pervasive changes to communication between organizations, communities, and individuals.
Focus group	A focus group is a form of qualitative research in which a group of people are asked about their perceptions, opinions, beliefs, and attitudes towards a product, service, concept, advertisement, idea, or packaging. Questions are asked in an interactive group setting where participants are free to talk with other group members. The first focus group was held in Ernest Dichter's house in a room he built above his garage.
Industry classification	Industry classification or industry taxonomy organizes companies into industrial groupings based on similar production processes, similar products, or similar behavior in financial markets. A wide variety of taxonomies is in use, sponsored by different organizations and based on different criteria. [1]The NAICS Index File lists 19745 rubrics beyond the 6 digits which are not assigned codes.
Observational research	In marketing and the social sciences, observational research is a social research technique that involves the direct observation of phenomena in their natural setting. This differentiates it from experimental research in which a quasi-artificial environment is created to control for spurious factors, and where at least one of the variables is manipulated as part of the experiment.
Primary data	Raw data (also known as primary data) is a term for data collected from a source. Raw data has not been subjected to processing or any other manipulation, and are also referred to as primary data. Raw data is a relative term .
Secondary data	Secondary data, is data collected by someone other than the user. Common sources of secondary data for social science include censuses, organisational records and data collected through qualitative methodologies or qualitative research. Primary data, by contrast, are collected by the investigator conducting the research.
Survey research	Survey research is often used to assess thoughts, opinions, and feelings. Survey research can be specific and limited, or it can have more global, widespread goals. Today, survey research is used by a variety of different groups.
Galvanometer	A galvanometer is a type of sensitive ammeter: an instrument for detecting electric current.

3. Capturing Marketing Insights and Forecasting Demand

CHAPTER HIGHLIGHTS & NOTES: KEY TERMS, PEOPLE, PLACES, CONCEPTS

	It is an analog electromechanical actuator that produces a rotary deflection of some type of pointer in response to electric current through its coil in a magnetic field.
	Galvanometers were the first instruments used to detect and measure electric currents.
QR code	QR code is the trademark for a type of matrix barcode (or two-dimensional barcode) first designed for the automotive industry in Japan. A barcode is a machine-readable optical label that contains information about the item to which it is attached. A QR code uses four standardized encoding modes (numeric, alphanumeric, byte / binary, and kanji) to efficiently store data; extensions may also be used.
Questionnaire	A questionnaire is a research instrument consisting of a series of questions and other prompts for the purpose of gathering information from respondents. Although they are often designed for statistical analysis of the responses, this is not always the case. The questionnaire was invented by Sir Francis Galton.
Tachistoscope	A tachistoscope is a device that displays an image for a specific amount of time. It can be used to increase recognition speed, to show something too fast to be consciously recognized, or to test which elements of an image are memorable. Projection tachistoscopes use a slide or transparency projector equipped with the mechanical shutter system typical of a camera.
Data collection	Data collection is the process of gathering and measuring information on variables of interest, in an established systematic fashion that enables one to answer stated research questions, test hypotheses, and evaluate outcomes. The data collection component of research is common to all fields of study including physical and social sciences, humanities, business, etc. While methods vary by discipline, the emphasis on ensuring accurate and honest collection remains the same.
Forecasting	Forecasting is the process of making statements about events whose actual outcomes have not yet been observed. A commonplace example might be estimation of some variable of interest at some specified future date. Prediction is a similar, but more general term.
Sales	A sale is the act of selling a product or service in return for money or other compensation. Signalling completion of the prospective stage, it is the beginning of an engagement between customer and vendor or the extension of that engagement.
	The seller or salesperson - the provider of the goods or services - completes a sale in response to an acquisition or to an appropriation or to a request.
Market share	'Market share is the percentage of a market accounted for by a specific entity.' In a survey of nearly 200 senior marketing managers, 67 percent responded that they found the 'dollar market share' metric very useful, while 61% found 'unit market share' very useful.

3. Capturing Marketing Insights and Forecasting Demand

CHAPTER HIGHLIGHTS & NOTES: KEY TERMS, PEOPLE, PLACES, CONCEPTS

	'Marketers need to be able to translate sales targets into market share because this will demonstrate whether forecasts are to be attained by growing with the market or by capturing share from competitors. The latter will almost always be more difficult to achieve.
Gross domestic product	Gross domestic product is defined by the Organisation for Economic Co-operation and Development (OECD) as 'an aggregate measure of production equal to the sum of the gross values added of all resident, institutional units engaged in production (plus any taxes, and minus any subsidies, on products not included in the value of their outputs).'
	Gross domestic product estimates are commonly used to measure the economic performance of a whole country or region, but can also measure the relative contribution of an industry sector. This is possible because Gross domestic product is a measure of 'value added' rather than sales; it adds each firm's value added (the value of its output minus the value of goods that are used up in producing it). For example, a firm buys steel and adds value to it by producing a car; double counting would occur if Gross domestic product added together the value of the steel and the value of the car.
Demographic	Demographics are the quantifiable statistics of a given population. Demographics are also used to identify the study of quantifiable subsets within a given population which characterize that population at a specific point in time.
	Demography is used widely in public opinion polling and marketing.
Diversity	In sociology and political studies, the term diversity is used to describe political entities (neighborhoods, student bodies, etc). with members who have identifiable differences in their cultural backgrounds or lifestyles.
	The term describes differences in racial or ethnic classifications, age, gender, religion, philosophy, physical abilities, socioeconomic background, sexual orientation, gender identity, intelligence, mental health, physical health, genetic attributes, behavior, attractiveness, or other identifying features.
Consumer	A consumer is a person or group of people, such as a household, who are the final users of products or services. The consumer's use is final in the sense that the product is usually not improved by the use.
Social network	A social network is a social structure made up of a set of social actors and a set of the dyadic ties between these actors. The social network perspective provides a set of methods for analyzing the structure of whole social entities as well as a variety of theories explaining the patterns observed in these structures.

3. Capturing Marketing Insights and Forecasting Demand

CHAPTER HIGHLIGHTS & NOTES: KEY TERMS, PEOPLE, PLACES, CONCEPTS

View	In database theory, a view is the result set of a stored query on the data, which the database users can query just as they would in a persistent database collection object. This pre-established query command is kept in the database dictionary. Unlike ordinary base tables in a relational database, a view does not form part of the physical schema: as a result set, it is a virtual table computed or collated dynamically from data in the database when access to that view is requested.
Innovation	Innovation is a new idea, device or process. Innovation can be viewed as the application of better solutions that meet new requirements, inarticulated needs, or existing market needs. This is accomplished through more effective products, processes, services, technologies, or ideas that are readily available to markets, governments and society.
Market testing	Concept testing (or market testing) is the process of using quantitative methods and qualitative methods to evaluate consumer response to a product idea prior to the introduction of a product to the market. It can also be used to generate communication designed to alter consumer attitudes toward existing products. These methods involve the evaluation by consumers of product concepts having certain rational benefits, such as 'a detergent that removes stains but is gentle on fabrics,' or non-rational benefits, such as 'a shampoo that lets you be yourself.' Such methods are commonly referred to as concept testing and have been performed using field surveys, personal interviews and focus groups, in combination with various quantitative methods, to generate and evaluate product concepts.

CHAPTER QUIZ: KEY TERMS, PEOPLE, PLACES, CONCEPTS

1. Concept testing (or _____) is the process of using quantitative methods and qualitative methods to evaluate consumer response to a product idea prior to the introduction of a product to the market. It can also be used to generate communication designed to alter consumer attitudes toward existing products. These methods involve the evaluation by consumers of product concepts having certain rational benefits, such as 'a detergent that removes stains but is gentle on fabrics,' or non-rational benefits, such as 'a shampoo that lets you be yourself.' Such methods are commonly referred to as concept testing and have been performed using field surveys, personal interviews and focus groups, in combination with various quantitative methods, to generate and evaluate product concepts.

    a. Market testing
    b. Canonical cover
    c. Chase
    d. Conjunctive query

2. . _____ refers to a range of technologies and techniques used by online website publishers and advertisers aimed at increasing the effectiveness of advertising using user web-browsing behavior information.

3. Capturing Marketing Insights and Forecasting Demand

CHAPTER QUIZ: KEY TERMS, PEOPLE, PLACES, CONCEPTS

In particular, '_____ uses information collected from an individual's web-browsing behavior (e.g., the pages that they have visited or the searches they have conducted) to select advertisements to display'.

When a consumer visits a web site, the pages they visit, the amount of time they view each page, the links they click on, the searches they make and the things that they interact with, allow sites to collect that data, and other factors, create a 'profile' that links to that visitor's web browser.

a. Behavioral retargeting
b. Total Immersion
c. Billboard
d. Behavioral targeting

3. _____ is a blanket term for any collection of data sets so large and complex that it becomes difficult to process using on-hand database management tools or traditional data processing applications.

The challenges include capture, curation, storage, search, sharing, transfer, analysis and visualization. The trend to larger data sets is due to the additional information derivable from analysis of a single large set of related data, as compared to separate smaller sets with the same total amount of data, allowing correlations to be found to 'spot business trends, determine quality of research, prevent diseases, link legal citations, combat crime, and determine real-time roadway traffic conditions.'

Scientists regularly encounter limitations due to large data sets in many areas, including meteorology, genomics, connectomics, complex physics simulations, and biological and environmental research.

a. Data archaeology
b. Data management
c. Big data
d. Business process preservation

4. _____ is the social interaction among people in which they create, share or exchange information and ideas in virtual communities and networks. Andreas Kaplan and Michael Haenlein define _____ as 'a group of Internet-based applications that build on the ideological and technological foundations of Web 2.0, and that allow the creation and exchange of user-generated content.' Furthermore, _____ depend on mobile and web-based technologies to create highly interactive platforms through which individuals and communities share, co-create, discuss, and modify user-generated content. They introduce substantial and pervasive changes to communication between organizations, communities, and individuals.

a. Strategy of tension
b. Tulip mania
c. Millenary Petition
d. Social media

3. Capturing Marketing Insights and Forecasting Demand

CHAPTER QUIZ: KEY TERMS, PEOPLE, PLACES, CONCEPTS

5. _____, an interdisciplinary subfield of computer science, is the computational process of discovering patterns in large data sets involving methods at the intersection of artificial intelligence, machine learning, statistics, and database systems. The overall goal of the _____ process is to extract information from a data set and transform it into an understandable structure for further use. Aside from the raw analysis step, it involves database and data management aspects, data pre-processing, model and inference considerations, interestingness metrics, complexity considerations, post-processing of discovered structures, visualization, and online updating.

   a. 1.96
   b. Data mining
   c. Bootstrapping
   d. Collocation

ANSWER KEY
3. Capturing Marketing Insights and Forecasting Demand

1. a
2. d
3. c
4. d
5. b

You can take the complete Chapter Practice Test

for 3. Capturing Marketing Insights and Forecasting Demand
on all key terms, persons, places, and concepts.

Online 99 Cents

http://www.JustTheFacts101.com

Use www.JustTheFacts101.com for all your study needs

including Facts101's online interactive problem solving labs in

chemistry, statistics, mathematics, and more.

4. Creating Long-Term Loyalty Relationships

CHAPTER OUTLINE: KEY TERMS, PEOPLE, PLACES, CONCEPTS

_____ Customer satisfaction

_____ Customer

_____ Customer-perceived value

_____ Value proposition

_____ QR code

_____ Customer profitability

_____ Product

_____ Performance

_____ Customer lifetime value

_____ Customer relationship management

_____ Permission marketing

_____ Social marketing

_____ Loyalty program

4. Creating Long-Term Loyalty Relationships

CHAPTER HIGHLIGHTS & NOTES: KEY TERMS, PEOPLE, PLACES, CONCEPTS

Customer satisfaction	'Customer satisfaction is a term frequently used in marketing. It is a measure of how products and services supplied by a company meet or surpass customer expectation. Customer satisfaction is defined as 'the number of customers, or percentage of total customers, whose reported experience with a firm, its products, or its services (ratings) exceeds specified satisfaction goals.' In a survey of nearly 200 senior marketing managers, 71 percent responded that they found a customer satisfaction metric very useful in managing and monitoring their businesses.
Customer	A customer is the recipient of a good, service, product, or idea, obtained from a seller, vendor, or supplier for a monetary or other valuable consideration. Customers are generally categorized into two types:•An intermediate customer or trade customer who is a dealer that purchases goods for re-sale.•An ultimate customer who does not in turn re-sell the things bought but either passes them to the consumer or actually is the consumer. A customer may or may not also be a consumer, but the two notions are distinct, even though the terms are commonly confused. A customer purchases goods; a consumer uses them.
Customer-perceived value	Value in marketing, also known as customer-perceived value, is the difference between a prospective customer's evaluation of the benefits and costs of one product when compared with others. Value may also be expressed as a straightforward relationship between perceived benefits and perceived costs: Value = Benefits / Cost. The customers get benefits and assume costs.
Value proposition	A value proposition is a promise of value to be delivered and acknowledged and a belief from the customer that value will be delivered and experienced. A value proposition can apply to an entire organization, or parts thereof, or customer accounts, or products or services. Creating a value proposition is a part of business strategy.
QR code	QR code is the trademark for a type of matrix barcode (or two-dimensional barcode) first designed for the automotive industry in Japan. A barcode is a machine-readable optical label that contains information about the item to which it is attached. A QR code uses four standardized encoding modes (numeric, alphanumeric, byte / binary, and kanji) to efficiently store data; extensions may also be used.
Customer profitability	Customer profitability is the profit the firm makes from serving a customer or customer group over a specified period of time, specifically the difference between the revenues earned from and the costs associated with the customer relationship in a specified period. According to Philip Kotler,'a profitable customer is a person, household or a company that overtime, yields a revenue stream that exceeds by an acceptable amount the company's cost stream of attracting, selling and servicing the customer.'

4. Creating Long-Term Loyalty Relationships

CHAPTER HIGHLIGHTS & NOTES: KEY TERMS, PEOPLE, PLACES, CONCEPTS

	Calculating customer profit is an important step in understanding which customer relationships are better than others. Often, the firm will find that some customer relationships are unprofitable.
Product	In marketing, a product is anything that can be offered to a market that might satisfy a want or need. In retailing, products are called merchandise. In manufacturing, products are bought as raw materials and sold as finished goods.
Performance	A performance, in performing arts, generally comprises an event in which a performer or group of performers behave in a particular way for another group of people, the audience. Choral music and ballet are examples. Usually the performers participate in rehearsals beforehand.
Customer lifetime value	In marketing, customer lifetime value lifetime customer value (LCV), or user lifetime value (LTV) is a prediction of the net profit attributed to the entire future relationship with a customer. The prediction model can have varying levels of sophistication and accuracy, ranging from a crude heuristic to the use of complex predictive analytics techniques.
	Customer lifetime value can also be defined as the dollar value of a customer relationship, based on the present value of the projected future cash flows from the customer relationship.
Customer relationship management	Customer relationship management is a system for managing a company's interactions with current and future customers. It involves using technology to organize, automate and synchronize sales, marketing, customer service, and technical support.
Permission marketing	Permission marketing is a term popularized by Seth Godin used in marketing in general and e-marketing specifically. The undesirable opposite of permission marketing is interruption marketing. Marketers obtain permission before advancing to the next step in the purchasing process.
Social marketing	Social marketing seeks to develop and integrate marketing concepts with other approaches to influence behaviors that benefit individuals and communities for the greater social good. It seeks to integrate research, best practice, theory, audience and partnership insight, to inform the delivery of competition sensitive and segmented social change programs that are effective, efficient, equitable and sustainable.
	Although 'social marketing' is sometimes seen only as using standard commercial marketing practices to achieve non-commercial goals, this is an oversimplification.
Loyalty program	Loyalty programs are structured marketing efforts that reward, and therefore encourage, loyal buying behavior - behavior which is potentially beneficial to the firm.

4. Creating Long-Term Loyalty Relationships

CHAPTER HIGHLIGHTS & NOTES: KEY TERMS, PEOPLE, PLACES, CONCEPTS

In marketing generally and in retailing more specifically, a loyalty card, rewards card, points card, advantage card, or club card is a plastic or paper card, visually similar to a credit card, debit card, or digital card that identifies the card holder as a member in a loyalty program. Loyalty cards are a system of the loyalty business model.

CHAPTER QUIZ: KEY TERMS, PEOPLE, PLACES, CONCEPTS

1. In marketing, a _____ is anything that can be offered to a market that might satisfy a want or need. In retailing, _____s are called merchandise. In manufacturing, _____s are bought as raw materials and sold as finished goods.

    a. Back to school
    b. Product
    c. Bass diffusion model
    d. Bayesian inference in marketing

2. _____ is the trademark for a type of matrix barcode (or two-dimensional barcode) first designed for the automotive industry in Japan. A barcode is a machine-readable optical label that contains information about the item to which it is attached. A _____ uses four standardized encoding modes (numeric, alphanumeric, byte / binary, and kanji) to efficiently store data; extensions may also be used.

    a. QR code
    b. Tulip mania
    c. Millenary Petition
    d. Contract of sale

3. Value in marketing, also known as _____, is the difference between a prospective customer's evaluation of the benefits and costs of one product when compared with others. Value may also be expressed as a straightforward relationship between perceived benefits and perceived costs: Value = Benefits / Cost.

    The customers get benefits and assume costs.

    a. Customer-perceived value
    b. reverse marketing
    c. Tulip mania
    d. Contract of sale

4. . '_____ is a term frequently used in marketing.

4. Creating Long-Term Loyalty Relationships

CHAPTER QUIZ: KEY TERMS, PEOPLE, PLACES, CONCEPTS

43

It is a measure of how products and services supplied by a company meet or surpass customer expectation. _____ is defined as 'the number of customers, or percentage of total customers, whose reported experience with a firm, its products, or its services (ratings) exceeds specified satisfaction goals.' In a survey of nearly 200 senior marketing managers, 71 percent responded that they found a _____ metric very useful in managing and monitoring their businesses.

a. Behavioral clustering
b. Blissful ignorance effect
c. Canadian Index of Consumer Confidence
d. Customer satisfaction

5. _____ is the profit the firm makes from serving a customer or customer group over a specified period of time, specifically the difference between the revenues earned from and the costs associated with the customer relationship in a specified period. According to Philip Kotler,'a profitable customer is a person, household or a company that overtime, yields a revenue stream that exceeds by an acceptable amount the company's cost stream of attracting, selling and servicing the customer.'

Calculating customer profit is an important step in understanding which customer relationships are better than others. Often, the firm will find that some customer relationships are unprofitable.

a. Bargain bin
b. Business to many
c. Category performance ratio
d. Customer profitability

ANSWER KEY
4. Creating Long-Term Loyalty Relationships

1. b
2. a
3. a
4. d
5. d

You can take the complete Chapter Practice Test

for 4. Creating Long-Term Loyalty Relationships
on all key terms, persons, places, and concepts.

Online 99 Cents

http://www.JustTheFacts101.com

Use www.JustTheFacts101.com for all your study needs including Facts101's online interactive problem solving labs in chemistry, statistics, mathematics, and more.

5. Analyzing Consumer and Business Markets

CHAPTER OUTLINE: KEY TERMS, PEOPLE, PLACES, CONCEPTS

_____ Customer

_____ Consumption

_____ Self-concept

_____ Laddering

_____ Perception

_____ Selective distortion

_____ Selective retention

_____ Discrimination

_____ Generalization

_____ Model

_____ Information overload

_____ Consumer

_____ Sources

_____ Attitude

_____ Advertising

_____ Availability heuristic

_____ Heuristic

_____ Prospect theory

_____ Business-to-business

_____ Marketing

_____ Service

5. Analyzing Consumer and Business Markets

CHAPTER OUTLINE: KEY TERMS, PEOPLE, PLACES, CONCEPTS

	E-procurement
	Variable cost
	Inventory
	Opportunism
	Trust

CHAPTER HIGHLIGHTS & NOTES: KEY TERMS, PEOPLE, PLACES, CONCEPTS

Customer	A customer is the recipient of a good, service, product, or idea, obtained from a seller, vendor, or supplier for a monetary or other valuable consideration. Customers are generally categorized into two types:•An intermediate customer or trade customer who is a dealer that purchases goods for re-sale.•An ultimate customer who does not in turn re-sell the things bought but either passes them to the consumer or actually is the consumer. A customer may or may not also be a consumer, but the two notions are distinct, even though the terms are commonly confused. A customer purchases goods; a consumer uses them.
Consumption	Consumption is a major concept in economics and is also studied by many other social sciences. Economists are particularly interested in the relationship between consumption and income, and therefore in economics the consumption function plays a major role. Different schools of economists define production and consumption differently.
Self-concept	One's self-concept is a collection of beliefs about oneself that includes elements such as academic performance, gender roles and sexuality, and racial identity. Generally, self-concept embodies the answer to 'Who am I?'. Self-concept is distinguishable from self-awareness, which refers to the extent to which self-knowledge is defined, consistent, and currently applicable to one's attitudes and dispositions.
Laddering	Laddering is an investment technique that requires investors to purchase multiple financial products with different maturity dates.

5. Analyzing Consumer and Business Markets

CHAPTER HIGHLIGHTS & NOTES: KEY TERMS, PEOPLE, PLACES, CONCEPTS

Perception	Perception is the organization, identification, and interpretation of sensory information in order to represent and understand the environment. All perception involves signals in the nervous system, which in turn result from physical or chemical stimulation of the sense organs. For example, vision involves light striking the retina of the eye, smell is mediated by odor molecules, and hearing involves pressure waves.
Selective distortion	Selective distortion is a term that refers to the tendency of people to interpret information in a way that will support what they already believe. This concept, along with selective attention and selective retention, makes it hard for marketers to get their message across and create good product perception. The selectivity hypothesis states that when a preference for a certain outcome exists, people will selectively distort evaluations of ambiguous, rather than unambiguous information in order to arrive at a conclusion that is preferred by the judge, but also easily justified as being fairly derived.
Selective retention	Selective retention, in relating to the mind, is the process when people more accurately remember messages that are closer to their interests, values and beliefs, than those that are in contrast with their values and beliefs, selecting what to keep in the memory, narrowing the informational flow. Such examples could include:•A person may gradually reflect more positively on their time at school as they grow older•A consumer might remember only the positive health benefits of a product they enjoy•People tending to omit problems and disputes in past relationships•A conspiracy theorist paying less attention to facts which do not aid their standpoint Outside of the theory of memory and mind: Selective retention may also be retaining of contractual agreements upon moving on in open politics or of physical phenotypes in eugenic methods of propagation of traits and features of a genome. Among other fields where action can impose a strata of creative limitation.
Discrimination	Discrimination is action that denies social participation or human rights to categories of people based on prejudice. This includes treatment of an individual or group based on their actual or perceived membership in a certain group or social category, 'in a way that is worse than the way people are usually treated'. It involves the group's initial reaction or interaction, influencing the individual's actual behavior towards the group or the group leader, restricting members of one group from opportunities or privileges that are available to another group, leading to the exclusion of the individual or entities based on logical or irrational decision making.
Generalization	A generalization of a concept is an extension of the concept to less-specific criteria. It is a foundational element of logic and human reasoning. Generalizations posit the existence of a domain or set of elements, as well as one or more common characteristics shared by those elements.

5. Analyzing Consumer and Business Markets

CHAPTER HIGHLIGHTS & NOTES: KEY TERMS, PEOPLE, PLACES, CONCEPTS

Model	A model, is a person in a role either to promote, display, or advertise commercial products (notably fashion clothing) or to serve as a visual aide for people who are creating works of art. Modelling ('modeling' in American English) is considered to be different from other types of public performance, such as an acting, dancing or being a mime artist. The boundary between modelling and performing is, however, not well defined, although such activities as appearing in a movie or a play are almost never labelled as modelling.
Information overload	Information overload refers to the difficulty a person can have understanding an issue and making decisions that can be caused by the presence of too much information. The term is popularized by Alvin Toffler in his bestselling 1970 book Future Shock, but is mentioned in a 1964 book by Bertram Gross, The Managing of Organizations. Speier et al. (1999) stated:"Information overload occurs when the amount of input to a system exceeds its processing capacity.
Consumer	A consumer is a person or group of people, such as a household, who are the final users of products or services. The consumer's use is final in the sense that the product is usually not improved by the use.
Sources	Sources is a web portal for journalists, freelance writers, editors, authors and researchers, focusing especially on human sources: experts and spokespersons who are prepared to answer Reporters' questions or make themselves available for on-air interviews.
Attitude	In heraldry, an attitude is the position in which an animal, fictional beast, mythical creature, human or human-like being is emblazoned as a charge, supporter or crest. Many attitudes apply only to predatory beasts and are exemplified by the beast most frequently found in heraldry--the lion. Some other terms apply only to docile animals, such as the doe.
Advertising	Advertising or advertizing in business is a form of marketing communication used to encourage, persuade, or manipulate an audience to take or continue to take some action. Most commonly, the desired result is to drive consumer behavior with respect to a commercial offering, although political and ideological advertising is also common. This type of work belongs to a category called affective labor.
Availability heuristic	The availability heuristic is a mental shortcut that relies on immediate examples that come to a given person's mind when evaluating a specific topic, concept, method or decision. The availability heuristic operates on the notion that if something can be recalled, it must be important, or at least more important than alternative solutions which are not as readily recalled. Subsequently, under the availability heuristic people tend to heavily weigh their judgments toward more recent information, making new opinions biased toward that latest news.

5. Analyzing Consumer and Business Markets

CHAPTER HIGHLIGHTS & NOTES: KEY TERMS, PEOPLE, PLACES, CONCEPTS

Heuristic	A heuristic technique, sometimes called simply a heuristic, is any approach to problem solving, learning, or discovery that employs a practical methodology not guaranteed to be optimal or perfect, but sufficient for the immediate goals. Where finding an optimal solution is impossible or impractical, heuristic methods can be used to speed up the process of finding a satisfactory solution. For human beings heuristics can be mental shortcuts that ease the cognitive load of making a decision.
Prospect theory	Prospect theory is a behavioral economic theory that describes the way people choose between probabilistic alternatives that involve risk, where the probabilities of outcomes are known. The theory states that people make decisions based on the potential value of losses and gains rather than the final outcome, and that people evaluate these losses and gains using certain heuristics. The model is descriptive: it tries to model real-life choices, rather than optimal decisions.
Business-to-business	Business-to-business describes commerce transactions between businesses, such as between a manufacturer and a wholesaler, or between a wholesaler and a retailer. Contrasting terms are business-to-consumer (B2C) and business-to-government (B2G). B2B branding is a term used in marketing.
Marketing	Marketing is the process of communicating the value of a product or service to customers, for the purpose of selling that product or service. Marketing can be looked at as an organizational function and a set of processes for creating, delivering and communicating value to customers, and customer relationship management that also benefits the organization. Marketing is the science of choosing target markets through market analysis and market segmentation, as well as understanding consumer behavior and providing superior customer value.
Service	In economics, a service is an intangible commodity. That is, services are an example of intangible economic goods. Service provision is often an economic activity where the buyer does not generally, except by exclusive contract, obtain exclusive ownership of the thing purchased.
E-procurement	E-procurement is the business-to-business or business-to-consumer or business-to-government purchase and sale of supplies, work, and services through the Internet as well as other information and networking systems, such as electronic data interchange and enterprise resource planning. The e-procurement value chain consists of indent management, e-Tendering, e-Auctioning, vendor management, catalogue management, Purchase Order Integration, Order Status, Ship Notice, e-Invoicing, e-Payment, and contract management. Indent management is the workflow involved in the preparation of tenders.

5. Analyzing Consumer and Business Markets

51

CHAPTER HIGHLIGHTS & NOTES: KEY TERMS, PEOPLE, PLACES, CONCEPTS

Variable cost	Variable costs are costs that change in proportion to the good or service that a business produces. Variable costs are also the sum of marginal costs over all units produced. They can also be considered normal costs.
Inventory	Inventory or stock refers to the goods and materials that a business holds for the ultimate purpose of resale . Inventory management is a science primarily about specifying the shape and percentage of stocked goods. It is required at different locations within a facility or within many locations of a supply network to precede the regular and planned course of production and stock of materials.
Opportunism	Opportunism is the conscious policy and practice of taking selfish advantage of circumstances - with little regard for principles, or with what the consequences are for others. Opportunist actions are expedient actions guided primarily by self-interested motives. The term can be applied to individual humans and living organisms, groups, organizations, styles, behaviours, and trends.
Trust	A 'trust,' or 'corporate trust' is a large business. Originally, it was Standard Oil, which was already the largest corporation in the world

CHAPTER QUIZ: KEY TERMS, PEOPLE, PLACES, CONCEPTS

1. _____, in relating to the mind, is the process when people more accurately remember messages that are closer to their interests, values and beliefs, than those that are in contrast with their values and beliefs, selecting what to keep in the memory, narrowing the informational flow.

    Such examples could include:•A person may gradually reflect more positively on their time at school as they grow older•A consumer might remember only the positive health benefits of a product they enjoy•People tending to omit problems and disputes in past relationships•A conspiracy theorist paying less attention to facts which do not aid their standpoint

    Outside of the theory of memory and mind: _____ may also be retaining of contractual agreements upon moving on in open politics or of physical phenotypes in eugenic methods of propagation of traits and features of a genome. Among other fields where action can impose a strata of creative limitation.

    a. Memorization
    b. Tulip mania
    c. Selective retention
    d. Business contract hire

5. Analyzing Consumer and Business Markets

CHAPTER QUIZ: KEY TERMS, PEOPLE, PLACES, CONCEPTS

2. A _____, is a person in a role either to promote, display, or advertise commercial products (notably fashion clothing) or to serve as a visual aide for people who are creating works of art.

   Modelling ('modeling' in American English) is considered to be different from other types of public performance, such as an acting, dancing or being a mime artist. The boundary between modelling and performing is, however, not well defined, although such activities as appearing in a movie or a play are almost never labelled as modelling.

   a. Billboard
   b. Bibliography of advertising
   c. Bespoke Music
   d. Model

3. _____ is a behavioral economic theory that describes the way people choose between probabilistic alternatives that involve risk, where the probabilities of outcomes are known. The theory states that people make decisions based on the potential value of losses and gains rather than the final outcome, and that people evaluate these losses and gains using certain heuristics. The model is descriptive: it tries to model real-life choices, rather than optimal decisions.

   a. Behavioral clustering
   b. Prospect theory
   c. Canadian Index of Consumer Confidence
   d. Center for a New American Dream

4. A '_____,' or 'corporate _____' is a large business. Originally, it was Standard Oil, which was already the largest corporation in the world

   a. Bilateral monopoly
   b. Trust
   c. Chamberlinian monopolistic competition
   d. Coercive monopoly

5. _____ is an investment technique that requires investors to purchase multiple financial products with different maturity dates.

   a. National Investor Relations Institute
   b. Tulip mania
   c. Laddering
   d. Business contract hire

ANSWER KEY
5. Analyzing Consumer and Business Markets

1. c
2. d
3. b
4. b
5. c

You can take the complete Chapter Practice Test

for 5. Analyzing Consumer and Business Markets
on all key terms, persons, places, and concepts.

Online 99 Cents

http://www.JustTheFacts101.com

Use www.JustTheFacts101.com for all your study needs including Facts101's online interactive problem solving labs in chemistry, statistics, mathematics, and more.

6. Identifying Market Segments and Targets

CHAPTER OUTLINE: KEY TERMS, PEOPLE, PLACES, CONCEPTS

- Market segmentation
- Microsegment
- CLUSTER
- Demographic
- Advertising
- Generation X
- Market
- Diversity
- Multicultural marketing
- Psychographic
- Need
- Funnel
- Marketing
- Service
- Mass marketing
- Selective retention
- Big data
- E-commerce
- Long tail
- Mass customization

6. Identifying Market Segments and Targets

CHAPTER HIGHLIGHTS & NOTES: KEY TERMS, PEOPLE, PLACES, CONCEPTS

Market segmentation	Market segmentation is a marketing strategy that involves dividing a broad target market into subsets of consumers who have common needs and priorities, and then designing and implementing strategies to target them. Market segmentation strategies may be used to identify the target customers, and provide supporting data for positioning to achieve a marketing plan objective. Businesses may develop product differentiation strategies, or an undifferentiated approach, involving specific products or product lines depending on the specific demand and attributes of the target segment.
Microsegment	A microsegment is an extremely precise division of a market, typically identified by marketers through advanced technology and techniques, such as data mining, artificial intelligence, and algorithms. These technologies and techniques are used to recognize and predict minute consumer spending and behavioral patterns. Once identified, microsegments can become the focus of personalized direct micromarketing campaigns.
CLUSTER	Consortium Linking Universities of Science and Technology for Education and Research (CLUSTER) is a collection of twelve European universities which focus on science and engineering. There are joint programs and student exchanges held between the universities.
Demographic	Demographics are the quantifiable statistics of a given population. Demographics are also used to identify the study of quantifiable subsets within a given population which characterize that population at a specific point in time. Demography is used widely in public opinion polling and marketing.
Advertising	Advertising or advertizing in business is a form of marketing communication used to encourage, persuade, or manipulate an audience to take or continue to take some action. Most commonly, the desired result is to drive consumer behavior with respect to a commercial offering, although political and ideological advertising is also common. This type of work belongs to a category called affective labor.
Generation X	Generation X, commonly abbreviated to Gen X, is the generation born after the Western Post-World War II baby boom. Demographers, historians, and commentators use beginning birth dates ranging from the early 1960s to the early 1980s.
Market	A market is one of the many varieties of systems, institutions, procedures, social relations and infrastructures whereby parties engage in exchange. While parties may exchange goods and services by barter, most markets rely on sellers offering their goods or services (including labor) in exchange for money from buyers. It can be said that a market is the process by which the prices of goods and services are established.

6. Identifying Market Segments and Targets

CHAPTER HIGHLIGHTS & NOTES: KEY TERMS, PEOPLE, PLACES, CONCEPTS

Diversity	In sociology and political studies, the term diversity is used to describe political entities (neighborhoods, student bodies, etc). with members who have identifiable differences in their cultural backgrounds or lifestyles. The term describes differences in racial or ethnic classifications, age, gender, religion, philosophy, physical abilities, socioeconomic background, sexual orientation, gender identity, intelligence, mental health, physical health, genetic attributes, behavior, attractiveness, or other identifying features.
Multicultural marketing	Multicultural marketing is the practice of marketing to one or more audiences of a specific ethnicity -- typically an ethnicity outside of a country's majority culture, which is sometimes called the 'general market.' Typically, multicultural marketing takes advantage of the ethnic group's different cultural referents -- such as language, traditions, celebrations, religion and any other concepts -- to communicate to and persuade that audience.
Psychographic	Psychographics is the study of personality, values, opinions, attitudes, interests, and lifestyles. Because this area of research focuses on interests, attitudes, and opinions, psychographic factors are also called IAO variables. Psychographic studies of individuals or communities can be valuable in the fields of marketing, demographics, opinion research, futuring, and social research in general.
Need	A need is something that is necessary for organisms to live a healthy life. Needs are distinguished from wants because a deficiency would cause a clear negative outcome, such as dysfunction or death. Needs can be objective and physical, such as food, or they can be subjective and psychological, such as the need for self-esteem.
Funnel	In Computer Science, a funnel is a synchronization primitive used in kernel development to protect system resources. First used on Digital UNIX as a way to 'funnel' device driver execution onto a single processor, funnels are now used in the Mac OS X kernel to serialize access to the BSD portion of xnu. A funnel is a mutex that prevents more than one thread from accessing certain kernel resources at the same time.
Marketing	Marketing is the process of communicating the value of a product or service to customers, for the purpose of selling that product or service. Marketing can be looked at as an organizational function and a set of processes for creating, delivering and communicating value to customers, and customer relationship management that also benefits the organization. Marketing is the science of choosing target markets through market analysis and market segmentation, as well as understanding consumer behavior and providing superior customer value.

6. Identifying Market Segments and Targets

CHAPTER HIGHLIGHTS & NOTES: KEY TERMS, PEOPLE, PLACES, CONCEPTS

Service	In economics, a service is an intangible commodity. That is, services are an example of intangible economic goods. Service provision is often an economic activity where the buyer does not generally, except by exclusive contract, obtain exclusive ownership of the thing purchased.
Mass marketing	Mass marketing is a market coverage strategy in which a firm decides to ignore market segment differences and appeal the whole market with one offer or one strategy. The idea is to broadcast a message that will reach the largest number of people possible. Traditionally mass marketing has focused on radio, television and newspapers as the media used to reach this broad audience.
Selective retention	Selective retention, in relating to the mind, is the process when people more accurately remember messages that are closer to their interests, values and beliefs, than those that are in contrast with their values and beliefs, selecting what to keep in the memory, narrowing the informational flow. Such examples could include:•A person may gradually reflect more positively on their time at school as they grow older•A consumer might remember only the positive health benefits of a product they enjoy•People tending to omit problems and disputes in past relationships•A conspiracy theorist paying less attention to facts which do not aid their standpoint Outside of the theory of memory and mind: Selective retention may also be retaining of contractual agreements upon moving on in open politics or of physical phenotypes in eugenic methods of propagation of traits and features of a genome. Among other fields where action can impose a strata of creative limitation.
Big data	Big data is a blanket term for any collection of data sets so large and complex that it becomes difficult to process using on-hand database management tools or traditional data processing applications. The challenges include capture, curation, storage, search, sharing, transfer, analysis and visualization. The trend to larger data sets is due to the additional information derivable from analysis of a single large set of related data, as compared to separate smaller sets with the same total amount of data, allowing correlations to be found to 'spot business trends, determine quality of research, prevent diseases, link legal citations, combat crime, and determine real-time roadway traffic conditions.' Scientists regularly encounter limitations due to large data sets in many areas, including meteorology, genomics, connectomics, complex physics simulations, and biological and environmental research.
E-commerce	Electronic commerce, commonly known as E-commerce or eCommerce, is trading in products or services using computer networks, such as the Internet.

6. Identifying Market Segments and Targets

CHAPTER HIGHLIGHTS & NOTES: KEY TERMS, PEOPLE, PLACES, CONCEPTS

	Electronic commerce draws on technologies such as mobile commerce, electronic funds transfer, supply chain management, Internet marketing, online transaction processing, electronic data interchange (EDI), inventory management systems, and automated data collection systems. Modern electronic commerce typically uses the World Wide Web for at least one part of the transaction's life cycle, although it may also use other technologies such as e-mail, mobile devices, social media, and telephones.
Long tail	In statistics, a long tail of some distributions of numbers is the portion of the distribution having a large number of occurrences far from the 'head' or central part of the distribution. The distribution could involve popularities, random numbers of occurrences of events with various probabilities, etc. A probability distribution is said to have a long tail, if a larger share of population rests within its tail than would under a normal distribution.
Mass customization	Mass customization, in marketing, manufacturing, call centres and management, is the use of flexible computer-aided manufacturing systems to produce custom output. Those systems combine the low unit costs of mass production processes with the flexibility of individual customization. Mass customization is the new frontier in business competition for both manufacturing and service industries.

CHAPTER QUIZ: KEY TERMS, PEOPLE, PLACES, CONCEPTS

1. In economics, a _____ is an intangible commodity. That is, _____s are an example of intangible economic goods.

   _____ provision is often an economic activity where the buyer does not generally, except by exclusive contract, obtain exclusive ownership of the thing purchased.

   a. Bad
   b. Service
   c. Case
   d. Club good

2. . _____ or advertizing in business is a form of marketing communication used to encourage, persuade, or manipulate an audience to take or continue to take some action. Most commonly, the desired result is to drive consumer behavior with respect to a commercial offering, although political and ideological _____ is also common. This type of work belongs to a category called affective labor.

   a. Advertising
   b. CloverETL

6. Identifying Market Segments and Targets

CHAPTER QUIZ: KEY TERMS, PEOPLE, PLACES, CONCEPTS

   c. Compuverde
   d. Continuuity

3. _____ is a blanket term for any collection of data sets so large and complex that it becomes difficult to process using on-hand database management tools or traditional data processing applications.

   The challenges include capture, curation, storage, search, sharing, transfer, analysis and visualization. The trend to larger data sets is due to the additional information derivable from analysis of a single large set of related data, as compared to separate smaller sets with the same total amount of data, allowing correlations to be found to 'spot business trends, determine quality of research, prevent diseases, link legal citations, combat crime, and determine real-time roadway traffic conditions.'

   Scientists regularly encounter limitations due to large data sets in many areas, including meteorology, genomics, connectomics, complex physics simulations, and biological and environmental research.

   a. Big data
   b. Data management
   c. Database normalization
   d. Business process preservation

4. In sociology and political studies, the term _____ is used to describe political entities (neighborhoods, student bodies, etc). with members who have identifiable differences in their cultural backgrounds or lifestyles.

   The term describes differences in racial or ethnic classifications, age, gender, religion, philosophy, physical abilities, socioeconomic background, sexual orientation, gender identity, intelligence, mental health, physical health, genetic attributes, behavior, attractiveness, or other identifying features.

   a. Diversity
   b. Christmas controversy
   c. Code word
   d. Collateral damage

5. Consortium Linking Universities of Science and Technology for Education and Research (_____) is a collection of twelve European universities which focus on science and engineering. There are joint programs and student exchanges held between the universities.

   a. 4C Entity
   b. Biometric Consortium
   c. CLUSTER
   d. Bonyad

ANSWER KEY
6. Identifying Market Segments and Targets

1. b
2. a
3. a
4. a
5. c

You can take the complete Chapter Practice Test

for 6. Identifying Market Segments and Targets
on all key terms, persons, places, and concepts.

Online 99 Cents

http://www.JustTheFacts101.com

Use www.JustTheFacts101.com for all your study needs including Facts101's online interactive problem solving labs in chemistry, statistics, mathematics, and more.

7. Crafting the Brand Positioning and Competing Effectively

CHAPTER OUTLINE: KEY TERMS, PEOPLE, PLACES, CONCEPTS

	Positioning
	Value proposition
	Market
	Market share
	Marketing myopia
	Competitor analysis
	Competitive advantage
	Emotional branding
	Brand
	Narrative
	Marketing
	Marketing research
	Social marketing
	Niche market
	Model
	Proactive
	Economic cost
	Adapter
	Imitation
	Innovation

7. Crafting the Brand Positioning and Competing Effectively

CHAPTER HIGHLIGHTS & NOTES: KEY TERMS, PEOPLE, PLACES, CONCEPTS

Positioning	Positioning is the marketing activity and process of identifying a market problem or opportunity, and developing a solution based on market research, segmentation and supporting data. Positioning may refer the position a business has chosen to carry out their marketing and business objectives. Positioning relates to strategy, in the specific or tactical development phases of carrying out an objective to achieve a business' or organization's goals, such as increasing sales volume, brand recognition, or reach in advertising.
Value proposition	A value proposition is a promise of value to be delivered and acknowledged and a belief from the customer that value will be delivered and experienced. A value proposition can apply to an entire organization, or parts thereof, or customer accounts, or products or services. Creating a value proposition is a part of business strategy.
Market	A market is one of the many varieties of systems, institutions, procedures, social relations and infrastructures whereby parties engage in exchange. While parties may exchange goods and services by barter, most markets rely on sellers offering their goods or services (including labor) in exchange for money from buyers. It can be said that a market is the process by which the prices of goods and services are established.
Market share	'Market share is the percentage of a market accounted for by a specific entity.' In a survey of nearly 200 senior marketing managers, 67 percent responded that they found the 'dollar market share' metric very useful, while 61% found 'unit market share' very useful. 'Marketers need to be able to translate sales targets into market share because this will demonstrate whether forecasts are to be attained by growing with the market or by capturing share from competitors. The latter will almost always be more difficult to achieve.
Marketing myopia	Marketing myopia is a term used in marketing as well as the title of an important marketing paper written by Theodore Levitt. This paper was first published in 1960 in the Harvard Business Review, a journal of which he was an editor. Marketing Myopia suggests that businesses will do better in the end if they concentrate on meeting customers' needs rather than on selling products.
Competitor analysis	Competitor analysis in marketing and strategic management is an assessment of the strengths and weaknesses of current and potential competitors. This analysis provides both an offensive and defensive strategic context to identify opportunities and threats. Profiling coalesces all of the relevant sources of competitor analysis into one framework in the support of efficient and effective strategy formulation, implementation, monitoring and adjustment.
Competitive advantage	Competitive advantage occurs when an organization acquires or develops an attribute or combination of attributes that allows it to outperform its competitors. These attributes can include access to natural resources, such as high grade ores or inexpensive power, or access to highly trained and skilled personnel human resources.

7. Crafting the Brand Positioning and Competing Effectively

CHAPTER HIGHLIGHTS & NOTES: KEY TERMS, PEOPLE, PLACES, CONCEPTS

Emotional branding	Emotional branding is a term used within marketing communication that refers to the practice of building brands that appeal directly to a consumer's emotional state, needs and aspirations. Emotional branding is successful when it triggers an emotional response in the consumer, that is, a desire for the advertised brand (or product) that cannot fully be rationalized. Emotional brands have a significant impact when the consumer experiences a strong and lasting attachment to the brand comparable to a feeling of bonding, companionship or love.
Brand	Brand is the 'name, term, design, symbol, or any other feature that identifies one seller's product distinct from those of other sellers.' Brands are used in business, marketing, and advertising. Initially, livestock branding was adopted to differentiate one person's cattle from another's by means of a distinctive symbol burned into the animal's skin with a hot branding iron. A modern example of a brand is Coca-Cola which belongs to the Coca-Cola Company.
Narrative	A narrative is any fictional or nonfictional report of connected events, presented in a sequence of written or spoken words, and/or in a sequence of (moving) pictures. Narrative can be organized in a number of thematic and/or formal, stylistic categories: non-fiction (e.g. New Journalism, creative non-fiction, biography, and historiography); fictionalized accounts of historical events (e.g. anecdote, myth, and legend); and fiction proper (i.e. literature in prose, such as short stories and novels, and sometimes in poetry and drama, although in drama the events are primarily being shown instead of told). Narrative is found in all forms of human creativity and art, including speech, writing, songs, film, television, games, photography, theatre, roleplaying games and visual arts such as painting (with the modern art movements refusing the narrative in favor of the abstract and conceptual) that describes a sequence of events.
Marketing	Marketing is the process of communicating the value of a product or service to customers, for the purpose of selling that product or service. Marketing can be looked at as an organizational function and a set of processes for creating, delivering and communicating value to customers, and customer relationship management that also benefits the organization. Marketing is the science of choosing target markets through market analysis and market segmentation, as well as understanding consumer behavior and providing superior customer value.
Marketing research	Marketing research is 'the process or set of processes that links the consumers, customers, and end users to the marketer through information -- information used to identify and define marketing opportunities and problems; generate, refine, and evaluate marketing actions; monitor marketing performance; and improve understanding of marketing as a process. Marketing research specifies the information required to address these issues, designs the method for collecting information, manages and implements the data collection process, analyzes the results, and communicates the findings and their implications.'

7. Crafting the Brand Positioning and Competing Effectively

CHAPTER HIGHLIGHTS & NOTES: KEY TERMS, PEOPLE, PLACES, CONCEPTS

	It is the systematic gathering, recording, and analysis of qualitative and quantitative data about issues relating to marketing products and services. The goal of marketing research is to identify and assess how changing elements of the marketing mix impacts customer behavior.
Social marketing	Social marketing seeks to develop and integrate marketing concepts with other approaches to influence behaviors that benefit individuals and communities for the greater social good. It seeks to integrate research, best practice, theory, audience and partnership insight, to inform the delivery of competition sensitive and segmented social change programs that are effective, efficient, equitable and sustainable.
	Although 'social marketing' is sometimes seen only as using standard commercial marketing practices to achieve non-commercial goals, this is an oversimplification.
Niche market	A niche market is the subset of the market on which a specific product is focused. The market niche defines the product features aimed at satisfying specific market needs, as well as the price range, production quality and the demographics that is intended to impact. It is also a small market segment.
Model	A model, is a person in a role either to promote, display, or advertise commercial products (notably fashion clothing) or to serve as a visual aide for people who are creating works of art.
	Modelling ('modeling' in American English) is considered to be different from other types of public performance, such as an acting, dancing or being a mime artist. The boundary between modelling and performing is, however, not well defined, although such activities as appearing in a movie or a play are almost never labelled as modelling.
Proactive	In organizational behavior and industrial/organizational psychology, proactivity or proactive behavior by individuals refers to anticipatory, change-oriented and self-initiated behavior in situations, particularly in the workplace. Proactive behavior involves acting in advance of a future situation, rather than just reacting. It means taking control and making things happen rather than just adjusting to a situation or waiting for something to happen.
Economic cost	The economic cost of a decision depends on both the cost of the alternative chosen and the benefit that the best alternative would have provided if chosen. Economic cost differs from accounting cost because it includes opportunity cost.
	As an example, consider the economic cost of attending college.
Adapter	An adapter or adaptor is a device that converts attributes of one electrical device or system to those of an otherwise incompatible device or system. Some modify power or signal attributes, while others merely adapt the physical form of one electrical connector to another.

7. Crafting the Brand Positioning and Competing Effectively

CHAPTER HIGHLIGHTS & NOTES: KEY TERMS, PEOPLE, PLACES, CONCEPTS

Imitation	Imitation is an advanced behavior whereby an individual observes and replicates another's behavior. Imitation is also a form of social learning that leads to the 'development of traditions, and ultimately our culture. It allows for the transfer of information (behaviours, customs, etc).
Innovation	Innovation is a new idea, device or process. Innovation can be viewed as the application of better solutions that meet new requirements, inarticulated needs, or existing market needs. This is accomplished through more effective products, processes, services, technologies, or ideas that are readily available to markets, governments and society.

CHAPTER QUIZ: KEY TERMS, PEOPLE, PLACES, CONCEPTS

1. _____ is the marketing activity and process of identifying a market problem or opportunity, and developing a solution based on market research, segmentation and supporting data. _____ may refer the position a business has chosen to carry out their marketing and business objectives. _____ relates to strategy, in the specific or tactical development phases of carrying out an objective to achieve a business' or organization's goals, such as increasing sales volume, brand recognition, or reach in advertising.

   a. Positioning
   b. Backward invention
   c. Bass diffusion model
   d. Bayesian inference in marketing

2. A _____ is a promise of value to be delivered and acknowledged and a belief from the customer that value will be delivered and experienced. A _____ can apply to an entire organization, or parts thereof, or customer accounts, or products or services.

   Creating a _____ is a part of business strategy.

   a. Value proposition
   b. Backward invention
   c. Bass diffusion model
   d. Bayesian inference in marketing

3. . A _____ is one of the many varieties of systems, institutions, procedures, social relations and infrastructures whereby parties engage in exchange. While parties may exchange goods and services by barter, most _____s rely on sellers offering their goods or services (including labor) in exchange for money from buyers. It can be said that a _____ is the process by which the prices of goods and services are established.

7. Crafting the Brand Positioning and Competing Effectively

CHAPTER QUIZ: KEY TERMS, PEOPLE, PLACES, CONCEPTS

   a. Total Immersion
   b. Barker channel
   c. 140 Proof
   d. Market

4. In organizational behavior and industrial/organizational psychology, proactivity or _____ behavior by individuals refers to anticipatory, change-oriented and self-initiated behavior in situations, particularly in the workplace. _____ behavior involves acting in advance of a future situation, rather than just reacting. It means taking control and making things happen rather than just adjusting to a situation or waiting for something to happen.

   a. Participatory management
   b. Tulip mania
   c. Proactive
   d. Barker channel

5. The _____ of a decision depends on both the cost of the alternative chosen and the benefit that the best alternative would have provided if chosen. _____ differs from accounting cost because it includes opportunity cost.

   As an example, consider the _____ of attending college.

   a. Economic cost
   b. Cost
   c. Cost accounting
   d. Cost curve

ANSWER KEY
7. Crafting the Brand Positioning and Competing Effectively

1. a
2. a
3. d
4. c
5. a

You can take the complete Chapter Practice Test

for 7. Crafting the Brand Positioning and Competing Effectively
on all key terms, persons, places, and concepts.

Online 99 Cents

http://www.JustTheFacts101.com

Use www.JustTheFacts101.com for all your study needs including Facts101's online interactive problem solving labs in chemistry, statistics, mathematics, and more.

8. Creating Brand Equity and Driving Growth

CHAPTER OUTLINE: KEY TERMS, PEOPLE, PLACES, CONCEPTS

- Brand
- Brand loyalty
- Brand equity
- BrandZ
- Model
- Mission statement
- Slogan
- Integrated marketing
- Brand valuation
- Brand architecture
- Reinforcement
- Fighter brand
- Cannibalization
- Customer
- Customer equity
- Customer lifetime value
- Double jeopardy

8. Creating Brand Equity and Driving Growth

CHAPTER HIGHLIGHTS & NOTES: KEY TERMS, PEOPLE, PLACES, CONCEPTS

Brand	Brand is the 'name, term, design, symbol, or any other feature that identifies one seller's product distinct from those of other sellers.' Brands are used in business, marketing, and advertising. Initially, livestock branding was adopted to differentiate one person's cattle from another's by means of a distinctive symbol burned into the animal's skin with a hot branding iron. A modern example of a brand is Coca-Cola which belongs to the Coca-Cola Company.
Brand loyalty	Brand loyalty is where a person buys products from the same manufacturer repeatedly rather than from other suppliers. In a survey of nearly 200 senior marketing managers, 68 percent responded that they found the 'loyalty' metric very useful.
Brand equity	Brand equity is a phrase used in the marketing industry which describes the value of having a well-known brand name, based on the idea that the owner of a well-known brand name can generate more money from products with that brand name than from products with a less well known name, as consumers believe that a product with a well-known name is better than products with less well-known names. Some marketing researchers have concluded that brands are one of the most valuable assets a company has, as brand equity is one of the factors which can increase the financial value of a brand to the brand owner, although not the only one. Elements that can be included in the valuation of brand equity include (but not limited to): changing market share, profit margins, consumer recognition of logos and other visual elements, brand language associations made by consumers, consumers' perceptions of quality and other relevant brand values.
BrandZ	BrandZ is Millward Brown's brand equity database. It holds data from over 650,000 consumers and professionals across 31 countries, comparing over 23,000 brands. The database is used to estimate brand valuations, and each year since 2006, has been used to generate a list of the top 100 global brands.
Model	A model, is a person in a role either to promote, display, or advertise commercial products (notably fashion clothing) or to serve as a visual aide for people who are creating works of art. Modelling ('modeling' in American English) is considered to be different from other types of public performance, such as an acting, dancing or being a mime artist. The boundary between modelling and performing is, however, not well defined, although such activities as appearing in a movie or a play are almost never labelled as modelling.
Mission statement	A mission statement is a statement of the purpose of a company, organization or person, its reason for existing.

8. Creating Brand Equity and Driving Growth

CHAPTER HIGHLIGHTS & NOTES: KEY TERMS, PEOPLE, PLACES, CONCEPTS

	The mission statement should guide the actions of the organization, spell out its overall goal, provide a path, and guide decision-making. It provides 'the framework or context within which the company's strategies are formulated.' It's like a goal for what the company wants to do for the world.
Slogan	A slogan is a memorable motto or phrase used in a political, commercial, religious, and other context as a repetitive expression of an idea or purpose. The word slogan is derived from slogorn which was an Anglicisation of the Scottish Gaelic and Irish sluagh-ghairm tanmay (sluagh 'army', 'host' + gairm 'cry'). Slogans vary from the written and the visual to the chanted and the vulgar.
Integrated marketing	Integrated Marketing Communication is the application of consistent brand messaging across both traditional and non-traditional marketing channels and using different promotional methods to reinforce each other.
Brand valuation	Brand valuation is the job of estimating the total financial value of the brand. Like the valuation of any product, of self review, or conflicts of interest if those that value the brand also were involved in its creation. The ISO 10668 standard sets out the appropriate process of valuing brands, and sets out six key requirements:•transparency,•validity,•reliability,•sufficiency,•objectivity, and•financial, behavioural, and legal parameters. Brand valuation is distinguished from brand equity.
Brand architecture	Brand architecture is the structure of brands within an organizational entity. It is the way in which the brands within a company's portfolio are related to, and differentiated from, one another. The architecture should define the different leagues of branding within the organization; how the corporate brand and sub-brands relate to and support each other; and how the sub-brands reflect or reinforce the core purpose of the corporate brand to which they belong.
Reinforcement	In behavioral psychology, reinforcement is a consequence that will strengthen an organism's future behavior whenever that behavior is preceded by a specific antecedent stimulus. This strengthening effect may be measured as a higher frequency of behavior (e.g., pulling a lever more frequently), longer duration (e.g., pulling a lever for longer periods of time), greater magnitude (e.g., pulling a lever with greater force), or shorter latency (e.g., pulling a lever more quickly following the antecedent stimulus). Although in many cases a reinforcing stimulus is a rewarding stimulus which is 'valued' or 'liked' by the individual (e.g., money received from a slot machine, the taste of the treat, the euphoria produced by an addictive drug), this is not a requirement.
Fighter brand	In marketing, a fighter brand is a lower priced offering launched by a company to take on, and ideally take out, specific competitors that are attempting to under-price them.

8. Creating Brand Equity and Driving Growth

CHAPTER HIGHLIGHTS & NOTES: KEY TERMS, PEOPLE, PLACES, CONCEPTS

	Unlike traditional brands that are designed with target consumers in mind, fighter brands are created specifically to combat a competitor that is threatening to take market share away from a company's main brand.
	A related concept is the flanker brand, a term often found in the mobile phone industry.
Cannibalization	In marketing strategy, cannibalization refers to a reduction in sales volume, sales revenue, or market share of one product as a result of the introduction of a new product by the same producer.
	While this may seem inherently negative, in the context of a carefully planned strategy, it can be effective, by ultimately growing the market, or better meeting consumer demands. Cannibalization is a key consideration in product portfolio analysis.
Customer	A customer is the recipient of a good, service, product, or idea, obtained from a seller, vendor, or supplier for a monetary or other valuable consideration. Customers are generally categorized into two types:•An intermediate customer or trade customer who is a dealer that purchases goods for re-sale.•An ultimate customer who does not in turn re-sell the things bought but either passes them to the consumer or actually is the consumer.
	A customer may or may not also be a consumer, but the two notions are distinct, even though the terms are commonly confused. A customer purchases goods; a consumer uses them.
Customer equity	Customer equity is the total combined customer lifetime values of all of a company's customers.
Customer lifetime value	In marketing, customer lifetime value lifetime customer value (LCV), or user lifetime value (LTV) is a prediction of the net profit attributed to the entire future relationship with a customer. The prediction model can have varying levels of sophistication and accuracy, ranging from a crude heuristic to the use of complex predictive analytics techniques.
	Customer lifetime value can also be defined as the dollar value of a customer relationship, based on the present value of the projected future cash flows from the customer relationship.
Double jeopardy	Double jeopardy is an empirical law in marketing where, with few exceptions, the lower market share brands in a market have both far fewer buyers in a time period and also lower brand loyalty.
	The term was originally coined by social scientist William McPhee in 1963 who observed the phenomenon, first in awareness and liking scores for Hollywood actors, and later in behaviours . Shortly afterwards Andrew Ehrenberg discovered the Double Jeopardy law generalised to brand purchasing.

8. Creating Brand Equity and Driving Growth

CHAPTER QUIZ: KEY TERMS, PEOPLE, PLACES, CONCEPTS

1. In behavioral psychology, _____ is a consequence that will strengthen an organism's future behavior whenever that behavior is preceded by a specific antecedent stimulus. This strengthening effect may be measured as a higher frequency of behavior (e.g., pulling a lever more frequently), longer duration (e.g., pulling a lever for longer periods of time), greater magnitude (e.g., pulling a lever with greater force), or shorter latency (e.g., pulling a lever more quickly following the antecedent stimulus).

    Although in many cases a reinforcing stimulus is a rewarding stimulus which is 'valued' or 'liked' by the individual (e.g., money received from a slot machine, the taste of the treat, the euphoria produced by an addictive drug), this is not a requirement.

    a. Reinforcement
    b. Tulip mania
    c. Millenary Petition
    d. Postmodern marketing

2. _____ is a phrase used in the marketing industry which describes the value of having a well-known brand name, based on the idea that the owner of a well-known brand name can generate more money from products with that brand name than from products with a less well known name, as consumers believe that a product with a well-known name is better than products with less well-known names.

    Some marketing researchers have concluded that brands are one of the most valuable assets a company has, as _____ is one of the factors which can increase the financial value of a brand to the brand owner, although not the only one. Elements that can be included in the valuation of _____ include (but not limited to): changing market share, profit margins, consumer recognition of logos and other visual elements, brand language associations made by consumers, consumers' perceptions of quality and other relevant brand values.

    a. Product management
    b. Brand equity
    c. Big Data Partnership
    d. CloverETL

3. _____ is where a person buys products from the same manufacturer repeatedly rather than from other suppliers.

    In a survey of nearly 200 senior marketing managers, 68 percent responded that they found the 'loyalty' metric very useful.

    a. Barloworld Limited
    b. Boomerang Media
    c. Brand loyalty
    d. Brand aversion

4. . A _____ is a memorable motto or phrase used in a political, commercial, religious, and other context as a repetitive expression of an idea or purpose. The word _____ is derived from slogorn which was an Anglicisation of the Scottish Gaelic and Irish sluagh-ghairm tanmay (sluagh 'army', 'host' + gairm 'cry'). _____s vary from the written and the visual to the chanted and the vulgar.

8. Creating Brand Equity and Driving Growth

CHAPTER QUIZ: KEY TERMS, PEOPLE, PLACES, CONCEPTS

   a. Broadside
   b. Christine
   c. Slogan
   d. CollarCard

5. _____ is the total combined customer lifetime values of all of a company's customers.

   a. Back to school
   b. Backward invention
   c. Bass diffusion model
   d. Customer equity

ANSWER KEY
8. Creating Brand Equity and Driving Growth

1. a
2. b
3. c
4. c
5. d

You can take the complete Chapter Practice Test

for 8. Creating Brand Equity and Driving Growth
on all key terms, persons, places, and concepts.

Online 99 Cents

http://www.JustTheFacts101.com

Use www.JustTheFacts101.com for all your study needs

including Facts101's online interactive problem solving labs in

chemistry, statistics, mathematics, and more.

9. Setting Product Strategy and Introducing New Offerings

CHAPTER OUTLINE: KEY TERMS, PEOPLE, PLACES, CONCEPTS

	Brand
	Customer
	Price
	Product
	Quality
	Durable good
	Raw material
	Service
	Marketing plan
	Product differentiation
	Department store
	Durability
	Mailing list
	Reliability
	Delivery
	Consistency
	Big data
	Consumer
	Information overload
	Pricing
	Co-branding

9. Setting Product Strategy and Introducing New Offerings

CHAPTER OUTLINE: KEY TERMS, PEOPLE, PLACES, CONCEPTS

_____	Innovation
_____	Concept testing
_____	Product concept
_____	Rapid prototyping
_____	Advertising
_____	Marketing strategy
_____	Business analysis
_____	Positioning
_____	Market
_____	Commercialization
_____	Strategy
_____	Evolution

CHAPTER HIGHLIGHTS & NOTES: KEY TERMS, PEOPLE, PLACES, CONCEPTS

Brand	Brand is the 'name, term, design, symbol, or any other feature that identifies one seller's product distinct from those of other sellers.' Brands are used in business, marketing, and advertising. Initially, livestock branding was adopted to differentiate one person's cattle from another's by means of a distinctive symbol burned into the animal's skin with a hot branding iron. A modern example of a brand is Coca-Cola which belongs to the Coca-Cola Company.
Customer	A customer is the recipient of a good, service, product, or idea, obtained from a seller, vendor, or supplier for a monetary or other valuable consideration. Customers are generally categorized into two types:•An intermediate customer or trade customer who is a dealer that purchases goods for re-sale.•An ultimate customer who does not in turn re-sell the things bought but either passes them to the consumer or actually is the consumer.

9. Setting Product Strategy and Introducing New Offerings

CHAPTER HIGHLIGHTS & NOTES: KEY TERMS, PEOPLE, PLACES, CONCEPTS

	A customer may or may not also be a consumer, but the two notions are distinct, even though the terms are commonly confused. A customer purchases goods; a consumer uses them.
Price	In ordinary usage, price is the quantity of payment or compensation given by one party to another in return for goods or services. In modern economies, prices are generally expressed in units of some form of currency. (For commodities, they are expressed as currency per unit weight of the commodity, e.g. euros per kilogram).
Product	In marketing, a product is anything that can be offered to a market that might satisfy a want or need. In retailing, products are called merchandise. In manufacturing, products are bought as raw materials and sold as finished goods.
Quality	Quality in business, engineering and manufacturing has a pragmatic interpretation as the non-inferiority or superiority of something; it is also defined as fitness for purpose. Quality is a perceptual, conditional, and somewhat subjective attribute and may be understood differently by different people. Consumers may focus on the specification quality of a product/service, or how it compares to competitors in the marketplace.
Durable good	In economics, a durable good or a hard good is a good that does not quickly wear out, or more specifically, one that yields utility over time rather than being completely consumed in one use. Items like bricks could be considered perfectly durable goods, because they should theoretically never wear out. Highly durable goods such as refrigerators, cars, or mobile phones usually continue to be useful for three or more years of use, so durable goods are typically characterized by long periods between successive purchases.
Raw material	A raw material or feedstock is basic material used in the production of goods, finished products or intermediate materials that are themselves feedstock for finished products. As feedstock, the term connotes it is a bottleneck asset critical to the production of other products. For example, crude oil is a feedstock raw material providing finished products in the fuel, plastic, industrial chemical and pharmaceutical industries.
Service	In economics, a service is an intangible commodity. That is, services are an example of intangible economic goods. Service provision is often an economic activity where the buyer does not generally, except by exclusive contract, obtain exclusive ownership of the thing purchased.
Marketing plan	A marketing plan may be part of an overall business plan. Solid marketing strategy is the foundation of a well-written marketing plan.

9. Setting Product Strategy and Introducing New Offerings

CHAPTER HIGHLIGHTS & NOTES: KEY TERMS, PEOPLE, PLACES, CONCEPTS

Product differentiation	In economics and marketing, product differentiation is the process of distinguishing a product or service from others, to make it more attractive to a particular target market. This involves differentiating it from competitors' products as well as a firm's own products. The concept was proposed by Edward Chamberlin in his 1933 Theory of Monopolistic Competition.
Department store	A department store is a retail establishment with a building open to the public, offering a wide range of consumer goods. It typically allows shoppers to choose between multiple merchandise lines, at variable price points, in different product categories known as 'departments'. Department stores usually sell a variety of products, including clothing, furniture, home appliances, toys, cosmetics, gardening, toiletries, sporting goods, do it yourself, paint, and hardware and additionally select other lines of products such as food, books, jewelry, electronics, stationery, photographic equipment, baby needs, and pet supplies.
Durability	In database systems, durability is the ACID property which guarantees that transactions that have committed will survive permanently. For example, if a flight booking reports that a seat has successfully been booked, then the seat will remain booked even if the system crashes. Durability can be achieved by flushing the transaction's log records to non-volatile storage before acknowledging commitment.
Mailing list	A mailing list is a collection of names and addresses used by an individual or an organization to send material to multiple recipients. The term is often extended to include the people subscribed to such a list, so the group of subscribers is referred to as 'the mailing list', or simply 'the list'.
Reliability	Reliability in research methods concerns the quality of measurement. Reliability refers to the 'repeatability' or 'consistency' of research measures.
Delivery	Delivery is the process of transporting goods from a source location to a predefined destination. There are different delivery types. Cargo (physical goods) are primarily delivered via roads and railroads on land, shipping lanes on the sea and airline networks in the air.
Consistency	In database systems, a consistent transaction is one that starts with a database in a consistent state and ends with the database in a consistent state. Consistent state means that there is no violation of any integrity constraints. Consistency may temporarily be violated during execution of the transaction, but must be corrected before changes are permanently committed to the database.
Big data	Big data is a blanket term for any collection of data sets so large and complex that it becomes difficult to process using on-hand database management tools or traditional data processing applications.

9. Setting Product Strategy and Introducing New Offerings

CHAPTER HIGHLIGHTS & NOTES: KEY TERMS, PEOPLE, PLACES, CONCEPTS

	The challenges include capture, curation, storage, search, sharing, transfer, analysis and visualization. The trend to larger data sets is due to the additional information derivable from analysis of a single large set of related data, as compared to separate smaller sets with the same total amount of data, allowing correlations to be found to 'spot business trends, determine quality of research, prevent diseases, link legal citations, combat crime, and determine real-time roadway traffic conditions.' Scientists regularly encounter limitations due to large data sets in many areas, including meteorology, genomics, connectomics, complex physics simulations, and biological and environmental research.
Consumer	A consumer is a person or group of people, such as a household, who are the final users of products or services. The consumer's use is final in the sense that the product is usually not improved by the use.
Information overload	Information overload refers to the difficulty a person can have understanding an issue and making decisions that can be caused by the presence of too much information. The term is popularized by Alvin Toffler in his bestselling 1970 book Future Shock, but is mentioned in a 1964 book by Bertram Gross, The Managing of Organizations. Speier et al. (1999) stated:"Information overload occurs when the amount of input to a system exceeds its processing capacity.
Pricing	Pricing is the process of determining what a company will receive in exchange for its product or service. Pricing factors are manufacturing cost, market place, competition, market condition, brand, and quality of product. Pricing is also a key variable in microeconomic price allocation theory.
Co-branding	Co-branding refers to several different marketing arrangements: Co-branding, also called brand partnership, is when two companies form an alliance to work together, creating marketing synergy. As described in Co-Branding: The Science of Alliance: Co-branding is an arrangement that associates a single product or service with more than one brand name, or otherwise associates a product with someone other than the principal producer. The typical co-branding agreement involves two or more companies acting in cooperation to associate any of various logos, color schemes, or brand identifiers to a specific product that is contractually designated for this purpose.
Innovation	Innovation is a new idea, device or process. Innovation can be viewed as the application of better solutions that meet new requirements, inarticulated needs, or existing market needs. This is accomplished through more effective products, processes, services, technologies, or ideas that are readily available to markets, governments and society.

9. Setting Product Strategy and Introducing New Offerings

CHAPTER HIGHLIGHTS & NOTES: KEY TERMS, PEOPLE, PLACES, CONCEPTS

Concept testing	Concept testing is the process of using quantitative methods and qualitative methods to evaluate consumer response to a product idea prior to the introduction of a product to the market. It can also be used to generate communication designed to alter consumer attitudes toward existing products. These methods involve the evaluation by consumers of product concepts having certain rational benefits, such as 'a detergent that removes stains but is gentle on fabrics,' or non-rational benefits, such as 'a shampoo that lets you be yourself.' Such methods are commonly referred to as concept testing and have been performed using field surveys, personal interviews and focus groups, in combination with various quantitative methods, to generate and evaluate product concepts.
Product concept	Product concept is the understanding of the dynamics of the product in order to showcase the best qualities and maximum features of the product. Marketers spend a lot of time and research in order to target their attended audience. Marketers will look into a product concept before marketing a product towards their customers.
Rapid prototyping	Rapid prototyping is a group of techniques used to quickly fabricate a scale model of a physical part or assembly using three-dimensional computer aided design data. Construction of the part or assembly is usually done using 3D printing or 'additive layer manufacturing' technology. The first methods for rapid prototyping became available in the late 1980s and were used to produce models and prototype parts.
Advertising	Advertising or advertizing in business is a form of marketing communication used to encourage, persuade, or manipulate an audience to take or continue to take some action. Most commonly, the desired result is to drive consumer behavior with respect to a commercial offering, although political and ideological advertising is also common. This type of work belongs to a category called affective labor.
Marketing strategy	Marketing strategy is defined by David Aaker as a process that can allow an organization to concentrate its resources on the optimal opportunities with the goals of increasing sales and achieving a sustainable competitive advantage. Marketing strategy includes all basic and long-term activities in the field of marketing that deal with the analysis of the strategic initial situation of a company and the formulation, evaluation and selection of market-oriented strategies and therefore contribute to the goals of the company and its marketing objectives.
Business analysis	Business analysis is a research discipline of identifying business needs and determining solutions to business problems. Solutions often include a systems development component, but may also consist of process improvement, organizational change or strategic planning and policy development. The person who carries out this task is called a business analyst or BA.

9. Setting Product Strategy and Introducing New Offerings

CHAPTER HIGHLIGHTS & NOTES: KEY TERMS, PEOPLE, PLACES, CONCEPTS

Positioning	Positioning is the marketing activity and process of identifying a market problem or opportunity, and developing a solution based on market research, segmentation and supporting data. Positioning may refer the position a business has chosen to carry out their marketing and business objectives. Positioning relates to strategy, in the specific or tactical development phases of carrying out an objective to achieve a business' or organization's goals, such as increasing sales volume, brand recognition, or reach in advertising.
Market	A market is one of the many varieties of systems, institutions, procedures, social relations and infrastructures whereby parties engage in exchange. While parties may exchange goods and services by barter, most markets rely on sellers offering their goods or services (including labor) in exchange for money from buyers. It can be said that a market is the process by which the prices of goods and services are established.
Commercialization	Commercialization is the process or cycle of introducing a new product or production method into the market. Many technologies begin in the laboratory and are not practical for commercial use in their infancy. The development segment of the research and development spectrum requires time and money as systems are engineered that will make the product or method a paying commercial proposition.
Strategy	Strategy is a high level plan to achieve one or more goals under conditions of uncertainty. Strategy is important because the resources available to achieve these goals are usually limited. Strategy generally involves setting goals, determining actions to achieve the goals, and mobilizing resources to execute the actions.
Evolution	Evolution is an advertising campaign launched by Unilever in 2006 as part of its Dove Campaign for Real Beauty, to promote the newly created Dove Self-Esteem Fund. The centre of the Unilever campaign is a 75-second spot produced by Ogilvy & Mather in Toronto, Canada. The piece was first displayed online on 6 October 2006, and was later broadcast as a television and cinema spot in the Netherlands and the Middle East.

9. Setting Product Strategy and Introducing New Offerings

CHAPTER QUIZ: KEY TERMS, PEOPLE, PLACES, CONCEPTS

1. _____ refers to several different marketing arrangements:

   _____, also called brand partnership, is when two companies form an alliance to work together, creating marketing synergy. As described in _____: The Science of Alliance:

   _____ is an arrangement that associates a single product or service with more than one brand name, or otherwise associates a product with someone other than the principal producer. The typical _____ agreement involves two or more companies acting in cooperation to associate any of various logos, color schemes, or brand identifiers to a specific product that is contractually designated for this purpose.

   a. Broadside
   b. Co-branding
   c. The Best Job In The World
   d. 140 Proof

2. _____ is a research discipline of identifying business needs and determining solutions to business problems. Solutions often include a systems development component, but may also consist of process improvement, organizational change or strategic planning and policy development. The person who carries out this task is called a business analyst or BA.

   Business analysts whose work solely on developing software systems may be called IT business analysts, technical business analysts, online business analysts, business systems analysts, or systems analysts.

   a. 10,000ft
   b. Basis of estimate
   c. Business analysis
   d. Big Hairy Audacious Goal

3. _____ is the 'name, term, design, symbol, or any other feature that identifies one seller's product distinct from those of other sellers.' _____s are used in business, marketing, and advertising. Initially, livestock branding was adopted to differentiate one person's cattle from another's by means of a distinctive symbol burned into the animal's skin with a hot branding iron. A modern example of a _____ is Coca-Cola which belongs to the Coca-Cola Company.

   a. Back to school
   b. Backward invention
   c. Bass diffusion model
   d. Brand

4. . In economics, a _____ is an intangible commodity. That is, _____s are an example of intangible economic goods.

   _____ provision is often an economic activity where the buyer does not generally, except by exclusive contract, obtain exclusive ownership of the thing purchased.

   a. Bad

9. Setting Product Strategy and Introducing New Offerings

CHAPTER QUIZ: KEY TERMS, PEOPLE, PLACES, CONCEPTS

   b. Cargo
   c. Case
   d. Service

5. A _____ is one of the many varieties of systems, institutions, procedures, social relations and infrastructures whereby parties engage in exchange. While parties may exchange goods and services by barter, most _____s rely on sellers offering their goods or services (including labor) in exchange for money from buyers. It can be said that a _____ is the process by which the prices of goods and services are established.

   a. Market
   b. Barker channel
   c. 140 Proof
   d. Bespoke Music

ANSWER KEY
9. Setting Product Strategy and Introducing New Offerings

1. b
2. c
3. d
4. d
5. a

You can take the complete Chapter Practice Test

for 9. Setting Product Strategy and Introducing New Offerings
on all key terms, persons, places, and concepts.

Online 99 Cents

http://www.JustTheFacts101.com

Use www.JustTheFacts101.com for all your study needs

including Facts101's online interactive problem solving labs in

chemistry, statistics, mathematics, and more.

10. Designing and Managing Services

CHAPTER OUTLINE: KEY TERMS, PEOPLE, PLACES, CONCEPTS

- _____ Service
- _____ Retail
- _____ Inseparability
- _____ Intangibility
- _____ Marketing plan
- _____ Perishability
- _____ Physical evidence
- _____ Premium
- _____ Market
- _____ Demand management
- _____ Funnel
- _____ Services marketing
- _____ Yield management
- _____ Demand
- _____ Marketing
- _____ Customer
- _____ Attribution
- _____ Empowerment
- _____ Big data
- _____ Interactive marketing
- _____ Quality

10. Designing and Managing Services
CHAPTER OUTLINE: KEY TERMS, PEOPLE, PLACES, CONCEPTS

_____	Ingredient
_____	Innovation
_____	Convenience
_____	Data integration
_____	Product
_____	Need

CHAPTER HIGHLIGHTS & NOTES: KEY TERMS, PEOPLE, PLACES, CONCEPTS

Service	In economics, a service is an intangible commodity. That is, services are an example of intangible economic goods. Service provision is often an economic activity where the buyer does not generally, except by exclusive contract, obtain exclusive ownership of the thing purchased.
Retail	Retail is the sale of goods and services from individuals or businesses to the end-user. Retailers are part of an integrated system called the supply chain. A retailer purchases goods or products in large quantities from manufacturers directly or through a wholesale, and then sells smaller quantities to the consumer for a profit.
Inseparability	Inseparability is used in marketing to describe a key quality of services as distinct from goods. Inseparability is the characteristic that a service has which renders it impossible to divorce the supply or production of the service from its consumption. Other key characteristics of services include perishability, intangibility and variability.
Intangibility	Intangibility is used in marketing to describe the inability to assess the value gained from engaging in an activity using any tangible evidence. It is often used to describe services where there isn't a tangible product that the customer can purchase, that can be seen, tasted or touched. Other key characteristics of services include perishability, inseparability and variability.

10. Designing and Managing Services

CHAPTER HIGHLIGHTS & NOTES: KEY TERMS, PEOPLE, PLACES, CONCEPTS

Marketing plan	A marketing plan may be part of an overall business plan. Solid marketing strategy is the foundation of a well-written marketing plan. While a marketing plan contains a list of actions, a marketing plan without a sound strategic foundation is of little use.
Perishability	Perishability is used in marketing to describe the way in which service capacity cannot be stored for sale in the future. It is a key concept of services marketing. Other key characteristics of services include intangibility, inseparability and variability.
Physical evidence	Real evidence, material evidence or physical evidence is any material object, that play some actual role in the matter that gave rise to the litigation, introduced in a trial, intended to prove a fact in issue based on its demonstrable physical characteristics. Physical evidence can conceivably include all odd
Premium	Premiums are promotional items--toys, collectables, souvenirs and household products--that are linked to a product, and often require box tops, tokens or proofs of purchase to acquire. The consumer generally has to pay at least the shipping and handling costs to receive the premium. Premiums are sometimes referred to as prizes, although historically the word 'prize' has been used to denote (as opposed to a premium) an item that is packaged with the product (or available from the retailer at the time of purchase) and requires no additional payment over the cost of the product.
Market	A market is one of the many varieties of systems, institutions, procedures, social relations and infrastructures whereby parties engage in exchange. While parties may exchange goods and services by barter, most markets rely on sellers offering their goods or services (including labor) in exchange for money from buyers. It can be said that a market is the process by which the prices of goods and services are established.
Demand management	Demand management is a planning methodology used to manage and forecast the demand of products and services.
Funnel	In Computer Science, a funnel is a synchronization primitive used in kernel development to protect system resources. First used on Digital UNIX as a way to 'funnel' device driver execution onto a single processor, funnels are now used in the Mac OS X kernel to serialize access to the BSD portion of xnu. A funnel is a mutex that prevents more than one thread from accessing certain kernel resources at the same time.
Services marketing	Services marketing is a sub field of marketing which covers the marketing of both goods and services. Goods marketing includes the marketing of fast moving consumer goods (FMCG) and durables.

10. Designing and Managing Services

CHAPTER HIGHLIGHTS & NOTES: KEY TERMS, PEOPLE, PLACES, CONCEPTS

Yield management	Yield management is a variable pricing strategy, based on understanding, anticipating and influencing consumer behavior in order to maximize revenue or profits from a fixed, perishable resource . As a specific, inventory-focused branch of revenue management, yield management involves strategic control of inventory to sell it to the right customer at the right time for the right price. This process can result in price discrimination, where a firm charges customers consuming otherwise identical goods or services a different price for doing so.
Demand	In economics, demand is the utility for a good or service of an economic agent, relative to a budget constraint. (Note: This distinguishes 'demand' from 'quantity demanded', where demand is a listing or graphing of quantity demanded at each possible price. In contrast to demand, quantity demanded is the exact quantity demanded at a certain price.
Marketing	Marketing is the process of communicating the value of a product or service to customers, for the purpose of selling that product or service. Marketing can be looked at as an organizational function and a set of processes for creating, delivering and communicating value to customers, and customer relationship management that also benefits the organization. Marketing is the science of choosing target markets through market analysis and market segmentation, as well as understanding consumer behavior and providing superior customer value.
Customer	A customer is the recipient of a good, service, product, or idea, obtained from a seller, vendor, or supplier for a monetary or other valuable consideration. Customers are generally categorized into two types:•An intermediate customer or trade customer who is a dealer that purchases goods for re-sale.•An ultimate customer who does not in turn re-sell the things bought but either passes them to the consumer or actually is the consumer. A customer may or may not also be a consumer, but the two notions are distinct, even though the terms are commonly confused. A customer purchases goods; a consumer uses them.
Attribution	Attribution is the process of identifying a set of user actions that contribute in some manner to a desired outcome, and then assigning a value to each of these events. Marketing attribution provides a level of understanding of what combination of events influence individuals to engage in a desired behavior, typically referred to as a conversion.
Empowerment	Empowerment refers to increasing the economic, political, social, educational, gender, or spiritual strength of an entity or entities.
Big data	Big data is a blanket term for any collection of data sets so large and complex that it becomes difficult to process using on-hand database management tools or traditional data processing applications.

10. Designing and Managing Services

CHAPTER HIGHLIGHTS & NOTES: KEY TERMS, PEOPLE, PLACES, CONCEPTS

	The challenges include capture, curation, storage, search, sharing, transfer, analysis and visualization. The trend to larger data sets is due to the additional information derivable from analysis of a single large set of related data, as compared to separate smaller sets with the same total amount of data, allowing correlations to be found to 'spot business trends, determine quality of research, prevent diseases, link legal citations, combat crime, and determine real-time roadway traffic conditions.'
	Scientists regularly encounter limitations due to large data sets in many areas, including meteorology, genomics, connectomics, complex physics simulations, and biological and environmental research.
Interactive marketing	Interactive Marketing refers to the evolving trend in marketing whereby marketing has moved from a transaction-based effort to a conversation. John Deighton argued that interactive marketing features "the ability to address an individual and the ability to gather and remember the response of that individual" leading to "the ability to address the individual once more in a way that takes into account his or her unique response"(Deighton 1996). Interactive marketing is not synonymous with online marketing, although interactive marketing processes are facilitated by internet technology.
Quality	Quality in business, engineering and manufacturing has a pragmatic interpretation as the non-inferiority or superiority of something; it is also defined as fitness for purpose. Quality is a perceptual, conditional, and somewhat subjective attribute and may be understood differently by different people. Consumers may focus on the specification quality of a product/service, or how it compares to competitors in the marketplace.
Ingredient	An ingredient is a substance that forms part of a mixture . For example, in cooking, recipes specify which ingredients are used to prepare a specific dish. Many commercial products contain a secret ingredient that is purported to make them better than competing products.
Innovation	Innovation is a new idea, device or process. Innovation can be viewed as the application of better solutions that meet new requirements, inarticulated needs, or existing market needs. This is accomplished through more effective products, processes, services, technologies, or ideas that are readily available to markets, governments and society.
Convenience	Convenient procedures, products and services are those intended to increase ease in accessibility, save resources and decrease frustration. Convenience is a relative concept, and depends on context. For example, automobiles were once considered a convenience, yet today are regarded as a normal part of life.
Data integration	Data integration involves combining data residing in different sources and providing users with a unified view of these data.

10. Designing and Managing Services

CHAPTER HIGHLIGHTS & NOTES: KEY TERMS, PEOPLE, PLACES, CONCEPTS

	This process becomes significant in a variety of situations, which include both commercial (when two similar companies need to merge their databases) and scientific (combining research results from different bioinformatics repositories, for example) domains. Data integration appears with increasing frequency as the volume and the need to share existing data explodes.
Product	In marketing, a product is anything that can be offered to a market that might satisfy a want or need. In retailing, products are called merchandise. In manufacturing, products are bought as raw materials and sold as finished goods.
Need	A need is something that is necessary for organisms to live a healthy life. Needs are distinguished from wants because a deficiency would cause a clear negative outcome, such as dysfunction or death. Needs can be objective and physical, such as food, or they can be subjective and psychological, such as the need for self-esteem.

CHAPTER QUIZ: KEY TERMS, PEOPLE, PLACES, CONCEPTS

1. _____ is the process of communicating the value of a product or service to customers, for the purpose of selling that product or service.

   _____ can be looked at as an organizational function and a set of processes for creating, delivering and communicating value to customers, and customer relationship management that also benefits the organization.
   _____ is the science of choosing target markets through market analysis and market segmentation, as well as understanding consumer behavior and providing superior customer value.

   a. Back to school
   b. Marketing
   c. Bayesian inference in marketing
   d. Bass diffusion model

2. Real evidence, material evidence or _____ is any material object, that play some actual role in the matter that gave rise to the litigation, introduced in a trial, intended to prove a fact in issue based on its demonstrable physical characteristics. _____ can conceivably include all odd

   a. Tulip mania
   b. Physical evidence
   c. Category performance ratio
   d. Channel value proposition

10. Designing and Managing Services

CHAPTER QUIZ: KEY TERMS, PEOPLE, PLACES, CONCEPTS

3. In economics, a _____ is an intangible commodity. That is, _____s are an example of intangible economic goods.

   _____ provision is often an economic activity where the buyer does not generally, except by exclusive contract, obtain exclusive ownership of the thing purchased.

   a. Bad
   b. Cargo
   c. Service
   d. Club good

4. _____ involves combining data residing in different sources and providing users with a unified view of these data. This process becomes significant in a variety of situations, which include both commercial (when two similar companies need to merge their databases) and scientific (combining research results from different bioinformatics repositories, for example) domains. _____ appears with increasing frequency as the volume and the need to share existing data explodes.

   a. Data integration
   b. Bitmap index
   c. British Oceanographic Data Centre
   d. Business intelligence

5. _____ is used in marketing to describe a key quality of services as distinct from goods. _____ is the characteristic that a service has which renders it impossible to divorce the supply or production of the service from its consumption.

   Other key characteristics of services include perishability, intangibility and variability.

   a. Bargain bin
   b. Business to many
   c. Category performance ratio
   d. Inseparability

ANSWER KEY
10. Designing and Managing Services

1. b
2. b
3. c
4. a
5. d

You can take the complete Chapter Practice Test

for 10. Designing and Managing Services
on all key terms, persons, places, and concepts.

Online 99 Cents

http://www.JustTheFacts101.com

Use www.JustTheFacts101.com for all your study needs including Facts101's online interactive problem solving labs in chemistry, statistics, mathematics, and more.

11. Developing Pricing Strategies and Programs

CHAPTER OUTLINE: KEY TERMS, PEOPLE, PLACES, CONCEPTS

	Positioning
	Price
	Pricing strategies
	Consumption
	Pricing
	Advertising
	Pricing objectives
	Masstige
	Product
	Big data
	Demand
	Market share
	Cost
	Total cost
	Elasticity
	Fixed cost
	Price elasticity of demand
	Average cost
	Variable cost
	Markup
	Dutch auction

11. Developing Pricing Strategies and Programs

CHAPTER OUTLINE: KEY TERMS, PEOPLE, PLACES, CONCEPTS

- English auction
- High-low pricing
- Barter
- Funnel
- Geographical pricing
- Marketing
- Discounts and allowances
- Promotion
- Customer
- Event
- Price analysis
- Patronage
- Price discrimination
- Discounting
- Rebate

11. Developing Pricing Strategies and Programs

CHAPTER HIGHLIGHTS & NOTES: KEY TERMS, PEOPLE, PLACES, CONCEPTS

Positioning	Positioning is the marketing activity and process of identifying a market problem or opportunity, and developing a solution based on market research, segmentation and supporting data. Positioning may refer the position a business has chosen to carry out their marketing and business objectives. Positioning relates to strategy, in the specific or tactical development phases of carrying out an objective to achieve a business' or organization's goals, such as increasing sales volume, brand recognition, or reach in advertising.
Price	In ordinary usage, price is the quantity of payment or compensation given by one party to another in return for goods or services. In modern economies, prices are generally expressed in units of some form of currency. (For commodities, they are expressed as currency per unit weight of the commodity, e.g. euros per kilogram).
Pricing strategies	A business can use a variety of pricing strategies when selling a product or service. The Price can be set to maximize profitability for each unit sold or from the market overall. It can be used to defend an existing market from new entrants, to increase market share within a market or to enter a new market.
Consumption	Consumption is a major concept in economics and is also studied by many other social sciences. Economists are particularly interested in the relationship between consumption and income, and therefore in economics the consumption function plays a major role. Different schools of economists define production and consumption differently.
Pricing	Pricing is the process of determining what a company will receive in exchange for its product or service. Pricing factors are manufacturing cost, market place, competition, market condition, brand, and quality of product. Pricing is also a key variable in microeconomic price allocation theory.
Advertising	Advertising or advertizing in business is a form of marketing communication used to encourage, persuade, or manipulate an audience to take or continue to take some action. Most commonly, the desired result is to drive consumer behavior with respect to a commercial offering, although political and ideological advertising is also common. This type of work belongs to a category called affective labor.
Pricing objectives	Pricing objectives or goals give direction to the whole pricing process. Determining what your objectives are is the first step in pricing. When deciding on pricing objectives you must consider: 1) the overall financial, marketing, and strategic objectives of the company; 2) the objectives of your product or brand; 3) consumer price elasticity and price points; and 4) the resources you have available.
Masstige	Masstige is a marketing term meaning downward brand extension.

11. Developing Pricing Strategies and Programs

CHAPTER HIGHLIGHTS & NOTES: KEY TERMS, PEOPLE, PLACES, CONCEPTS

	The word is a portmanteau of the words mass and prestige and has been described as 'prestige for the masses' Masstige products are defined as 'premium but attainable,' and there are two key tenets: (1) They are considered luxury or premium products and (2) They have price points that fill the gap between mid-market and super premium. Silverstein and Fiske cite several examples:•Bath & Body Lotion that sells for $1.13 per ounce versus $0.30 per ounce.•Pottery Barn housewares that are considered premium but are widely available at attainable price points well below super premium brands.•Kendall-Jackson Wines that entered the market at $5 per bottle versus the standard $2 per bottle.•Porsche Boxster.
Product	In marketing, a product is anything that can be offered to a market that might satisfy a want or need. In retailing, products are called merchandise. In manufacturing, products are bought as raw materials and sold as finished goods.
Big data	Big data is a blanket term for any collection of data sets so large and complex that it becomes difficult to process using on-hand database management tools or traditional data processing applications. The challenges include capture, curation, storage, search, sharing, transfer, analysis and visualization. The trend to larger data sets is due to the additional information derivable from analysis of a single large set of related data, as compared to separate smaller sets with the same total amount of data, allowing correlations to be found to 'spot business trends, determine quality of research, prevent diseases, link legal citations, combat crime, and determine real-time roadway traffic conditions.' Scientists regularly encounter limitations due to large data sets in many areas, including meteorology, genomics, connectomics, complex physics simulations, and biological and environmental research.
Demand	In economics, demand is the utility for a good or service of an economic agent, relative to a budget constraint. (Note: This distinguishes 'demand' from 'quantity demanded', where demand is a listing or graphing of quantity demanded at each possible price. In contrast to demand, quantity demanded is the exact quantity demanded at a certain price.
Market share	'Market share is the percentage of a market accounted for by a specific entity.' In a survey of nearly 200 senior marketing managers, 67 percent responded that they found the 'dollar market share' metric very useful, while 61% found 'unit market share' very useful. 'Marketers need to be able to translate sales targets into market share because this will demonstrate whether forecasts are to be attained by growing with the market or by capturing share from competitors. The latter will almost always be more difficult to achieve.

11. Developing Pricing Strategies and Programs

CHAPTER HIGHLIGHTS & NOTES: KEY TERMS, PEOPLE, PLACES, CONCEPTS

Cost	In production, research, retail, and accounting, a cost is the value of money that has been used up to produce something, and hence is not available for use anymore. In business, the cost may be one of acquisition, in which case the amount of money expended to acquire it is counted as cost. In this case, money is the input that is gone in order to acquire the thing.
Total cost	In economics, and cost accounting, total cost describes the total economic cost of production and is made up of variable costs, which vary according to the quantity of a good produced and include inputs such as labor and raw materials, plus fixed costs, which are independent of the quantity of a good produced and include inputs (capital) that cannot be varied in the short term, such as buildings and machinery. Total cost in economics includes the total opportunity cost of each factor of production as part of its fixed or variable costs. The rate at which total cost changes as the amount produced changes is called marginal cost.
Elasticity	The elasticity of a data store relates to the flexibility of its data model and clustering capabilities. The greater the number of data model changes that can be tolerated, and the more easily the clustering can be managed, the more elastic the data store is considered to be.
Fixed cost	In economics, fixed costs, indirect costs or overheads are business expenses that are not dependent on the level of goods or services produced by the business. They tend to be time-related, such as salaries or rents being paid per month, and are often referred to as overhead costs. This is in contrast to variable costs, which are volume-related (and are paid per quantity produced).
Price elasticity of demand	Price elasticity of demand is a measure used in economics to show the responsiveness, or elasticity, of the quantity demanded of a good or service to a change in its price. More precisely, it gives the percentage change in quantity demanded in response to a one percent change in price (ceteris paribus, i.e. holding constant all the other determinants of demand, such as income). Price elasticities are almost always negative, although analysts tend to ignore the sign even though this can lead to ambiguity.
Average cost	In economics, average cost or unit cost is equal to total cost divided by the number of goods produced . It is also equal to the sum of average variable costs (total variable costs divided by Q) plus average fixed costs (total fixed costs divided by Q). Average costs may be dependent on the time period considered (increasing production may be expensive or impossible in the short term, for example).
Variable cost	Variable costs are costs that change in proportion to the good or service that a business produces. Variable costs are also the sum of marginal costs over all units produced. They can also be considered normal costs.

11. Developing Pricing Strategies and Programs

CHAPTER HIGHLIGHTS & NOTES: KEY TERMS, PEOPLE, PLACES, CONCEPTS

Markup	Markup is the difference between the cost of a good or service and its selling price. A markup is added onto the total cost incurred by the producer of a good or service in order to create a profit. The total cost reflects the total amount of both fixed and variable expenses to produce and distribute a product.
Dutch auction	A Dutch auction is a type of auction in which the auctioneer begins with a high asking price which is lowered until some participant is willing to accept the auctioneer's price, or a predetermined reserve price is reached. The winning participant pays the last announced price. This is also known as a clock auction or an open-outcry descending-price auction.
English auction	An English auction is a type of auction, whose most typical form is the 'open outcry' auction. The auctioneer opens the auction by announcing a Suggested Opening Bid, a starting price or reserve for the item on sale and then accepts increasingly higher bids from the floor consisting of buyers with a possible interest in the item. Unlike sealed bid auctions, 'open outcry' auctions are 'open' or fully transparent as the identity of all bidders is disclosed to each other during the auction.
High-low pricing	High-low pricing is a type of pricing strategy adopted by companies, usually small and medium sized retail firms. It is a type of pricing where a firm charges a high price for an item and later when the item's popularity has passed, sell it to customers by giving discounts or through clearance sales. The basic type of customers for the firms adopting high-low price will not have a clear idea about what a product's price would typically be or must have a strong belief that 'discount sales = low price' or they must have strong preference in purchasing the products sold in this type or by this certain firm.
Barter	Barter is a system of exchange by which goods or services are directly exchanged for other goods or services without using a medium of exchange, such as money. It is distinguishable from gift economies in that the reciprocal exchange is immediate and not delayed in time. It is usually bilateral, but may be multilateral (i.e., mediated through barter organizations) and usually exists parallel to monetary systems in most developed countries, though to a very limited extent.
Funnel	In Computer Science, a funnel is a synchronization primitive used in kernel development to protect system resources. First used on Digital UNIX as a way to 'funnel' device driver execution onto a single processor, funnels are now used in the Mac OS X kernel to serialize access to the BSD portion of xnu. A funnel is a mutex that prevents more than one thread from accessing certain kernel resources at the same time.
Geographical pricing	Geographical pricing, in marketing, is the practice of modifying a basic list price based on the geographical location of the buyer. It is intended to reflect the costs of shipping to different locations.

11. Developing Pricing Strategies and Programs

CHAPTER HIGHLIGHTS & NOTES: KEY TERMS, PEOPLE, PLACES, CONCEPTS

Marketing	Marketing is the process of communicating the value of a product or service to customers, for the purpose of selling that product or service. Marketing can be looked at as an organizational function and a set of processes for creating, delivering and communicating value to customers, and customer relationship management that also benefits the organization. Marketing is the science of choosing target markets through market analysis and market segmentation, as well as understanding consumer behavior and providing superior customer value.
Discounts and allowances	Discounts and allowances are reductions to a basic price of goods or services. They can occur anywhere in the distribution channel, modifying either the manufacturer's list price, the retail price (set by the retailer and often attached to the product with a sticker), or the list price (which is quoted to a potential buyer, usually in written form). There are many purposes for discounting, including; to increase short-term sales, to move out-of-date stock, to reward valuable customers, to encourage distribution channel members to perform a function, or to otherwise reward behaviors that benefit the discount issuer.
Promotion	Promotion is one of the market mix elements or features, and a term used frequently in marketing. The marketing mix includes the four P's: price, product, promotion, and place. Promotion refers to raising customer awareness of a product or brand, generating sales, and creating brand loyalty.
Customer	A customer is the recipient of a good, service, product, or idea, obtained from a seller, vendor, or supplier for a monetary or other valuable consideration. Customers are generally categorized into two types:•An intermediate customer or trade customer who is a dealer that purchases goods for re-sale.•An ultimate customer who does not in turn re-sell the things bought but either passes them to the consumer or actually is the consumer. A customer may or may not also be a consumer, but the two notions are distinct, even though the terms are commonly confused. A customer purchases goods; a consumer uses them.
Event	In computer science, an event is a type of synchronization mechanism that is used to indicate to waiting processes when a particular condition has become true. An event is an abstract data type with a boolean state and the following operations:•wait - when executed, causes the executing process to suspend until the event's state is set to true. If the state is already set to true has no effect.•set - sets the event's state to true, release all waiting processes.•clear - sets the event's state to false.

11. Developing Pricing Strategies and Programs

CHAPTER HIGHLIGHTS & NOTES: KEY TERMS, PEOPLE, PLACES, CONCEPTS

Price analysis	In marketing, Price Analysis refers to the analysis of consumer response to theoretical prices in survey research. In general business, Price Analysis is the process of examining and evaluating a proposed price without evaluating its separate cost elements and proposed profit/fee. Price analysis may also refer to the breakdown of a price to a unit figure.
Patronage	Patronage is the support, encouragement, privilege, or financial aid that an organization or individual bestows to another. In the history of art, arts patronage refers to the support that kings, popes and the wealthy have provided to artists such as musicians, painters, and sculptors. It can also refer to the right of bestowing offices or church benefices, the business given to a store by a regular customer, and the guardianship of saints.
Price discrimination	Price discrimination or price differentiation is a pricing strategy where identical or largely similar goods or services are transacted at different prices by the same provider in different markets or territories. Price differentiation is distinguished from product differentiation by the more substantial difference in production cost for the differently priced products involved in the latter strategy. Price differentiation essentially relies on the variation in the customers' willingness to pay.
Discounting	Discounting is a financial mechanism in which a debtor obtains the right to delay payments to a creditor, for a defined period of time, in exchange for a charge or fee. Essentially, the party that owes money in the present purchases the right to delay the payment until some future date. The discount, or charge, is the difference (expressed as a difference in the same units (absolute) or in percentage terms (relative), or as a ratio) between the original amount owed in the present and the amount that has to be paid in the future to settle the debt.
Rebate	A rebate is an amount paid by way of reduction, return, or refund on what has already been paid or contributed. It is a type of sales promotion that marketers use primarily as incentives or supplements to product sales. The mail-in rebate is the most common.

11. Developing Pricing Strategies and Programs

CHAPTER QUIZ: KEY TERMS, PEOPLE, PLACES, CONCEPTS

1. _____ or advertizing in business is a form of marketing communication used to encourage, persuade, or manipulate an audience to take or continue to take some action. Most commonly, the desired result is to drive consumer behavior with respect to a commercial offering, although political and ideological _____ is also common. This type of work belongs to a category called affective labor.

    a. Advertising
    b. CloverETL
    c. Compuverde
    d. Continuuity

2. _____ is the marketing activity and process of identifying a market problem or opportunity, and developing a solution based on market research, segmentation and supporting data. _____ may refer the position a business has chosen to carry out their marketing and business objectives. _____ relates to strategy, in the specific or tactical development phases of carrying out an objective to achieve a business' or organization's goals, such as increasing sales volume, brand recognition, or reach in advertising.

    a. Back to school
    b. Positioning
    c. Bass diffusion model
    d. Bayesian inference in marketing

3. In economics, _____ or unit cost is equal to total cost divided by the number of goods produced . It is also equal to the sum of average variable costs (total variable costs divided by Q) plus average fixed costs (total fixed costs divided by Q). _____s may be dependent on the time period considered (increasing production may be expensive or impossible in the short term, for example).

    a. Average cost
    b. Total Immersion
    c. Barker channel
    d. 140 Proof

4. . '_____ is the percentage of a market accounted for by a specific entity.' In a survey of nearly 200 senior marketing managers, 67 percent responded that they found the 'dollar _____' metric very useful, while 61% found 'unit _____' very useful.

    'Marketers need to be able to translate sales targets into _____ because this will demonstrate whether forecasts are to be attained by growing with the market or by capturing share from competitors. The latter will almost always be more difficult to achieve.

    a. Back to school
    b. Backward invention
    c. Market share

11. Developing Pricing Strategies and Programs

CHAPTER QUIZ: KEY TERMS, PEOPLE, PLACES, CONCEPTS

5. A business can use a variety of _____ when selling a product or service. The Price can be set to maximize profitability for each unit sold or from the market overall. It can be used to defend an existing market from new entrants, to increase market share within a market or to enter a new market.

   a. Back to school
   b. Backward invention
   c. Bass diffusion model
   d. Pricing strategies

ANSWER KEY
11. Developing Pricing Strategies and Programs

1. a
2. b
3. a
4. c
5. d

You can take the complete Chapter Practice Test

for 11. Developing Pricing Strategies and Programs
on all key terms, persons, places, and concepts.

Online 99 Cents

http://www.JustTheFacts101.com

Use www.JustTheFacts101.com for all your study needs including Facts101's online interactive problem solving labs in chemistry, statistics, mathematics, and more.

12. Designing and Managing Integrated Marketing Channels

CHAPTER OUTLINE: KEY TERMS, PEOPLE, PLACES, CONCEPTS

- E-commerce
- Marketing
- Multichannel marketing
- Marketing channel
- Pricing
- Strategy
- Demand chain
- Digital distribution
- Distribution
- Integrated marketing
- Digital marketing
- Delivery
- Flow
- Sales
- Service
- Direct marketing
- Customer
- Social marketing
- Need
- QR code
- Showrooming

12. Designing and Managing Integrated Marketing Channels
CHAPTER OUTLINE: KEY TERMS, PEOPLE, PLACES, CONCEPTS

	Agent
	Interactive marketing
	Merchant
	Horizontal marketing system
	Consumer
	Customer service
	Product
	Big data
	Channel conflict
	Advertising
	Promotion
	Shopping
	Cannibalization
	Co-optation
	Exclusive dealing
	Mediation
	Perception

12. Designing and Managing Integrated Marketing Channels

CHAPTER HIGHLIGHTS & NOTES: KEY TERMS, PEOPLE, PLACES, CONCEPTS

E-commerce	Electronic commerce, commonly known as E-commerce or eCommerce, is trading in products or services using computer networks, such as the Internet. Electronic commerce draws on technologies such as mobile commerce, electronic funds transfer, supply chain management, Internet marketing, online transaction processing, electronic data interchange (EDI), inventory management systems, and automated data collection systems. Modern electronic commerce typically uses the World Wide Web for at least one part of the transaction's life cycle, although it may also use other technologies such as e-mail, mobile devices, social media, and telephones.
Marketing	Marketing is the process of communicating the value of a product or service to customers, for the purpose of selling that product or service. Marketing can be looked at as an organizational function and a set of processes for creating, delivering and communicating value to customers, and customer relationship management that also benefits the organization. Marketing is the science of choosing target markets through market analysis and market segmentation, as well as understanding consumer behavior and providing superior customer value.
Multichannel marketing	Multichannel marketing is marketing using many different marketing channels to reach a customer. In this sense, a channel might be a retail store, a web site, a mail order catalogue, or direct personal communications by letter, email or text message. The objective of the companies doing the marketing is to make it easy for a consumer to buy from them in whatever way is most appropriate.
Marketing channel	A marketing channel is a set of practices or activities necessary to transfer the ownership of goods, and to move goods, from the point of production to the point of consumption and, as such, which consists of all the institutions and all the marketing activities in the marketing process. A marketing channel is a useful tool for management. Roles of marketing channel in marketing strategies•Links producers to buyers.•Performs sales, advertising and promotion.•Influences the firm's pricing strategy.•Affecting product strategy through branding, policies, willingness to stock.•Customizes profits, install, maintain, offer credit, etc..
Pricing	Pricing is the process of determining what a company will receive in exchange for its product or service. Pricing factors are manufacturing cost, market place, competition, market condition, brand, and quality of product. Pricing is also a key variable in microeconomic price allocation theory.
Strategy	Strategy is a high level plan to achieve one or more goals under conditions of uncertainty. Strategy is important because the resources available to achieve these goals are usually limited. Strategy generally involves setting goals, determining actions to achieve the goals, and mobilizing resources to execute the actions.

12. Designing and Managing Integrated Marketing Channels

CHAPTER HIGHLIGHTS & NOTES: KEY TERMS, PEOPLE, PLACES, CONCEPTS

Demand chain	The Demand chain is that part of the value chain which drives demand.
Digital distribution	Digital distribution describes the delivery or distribution of media content such as audio, video, software and video games usually over an online delivery medium, such as the Internet, without the use of physical media. Online distribution bypasses conventional physical distribution methods, such as paper, compact discs, and DVDs. The term online distribution is typically applied to freestanding products; downloadable add-ons for other products are more commonly known as downloadable content.
Distribution	Product distribution is one of the four elements of the marketing mix. Distribution is the process of making a product or service available for use or consumption by a consumer or business user, using direct means, or using indirect means with intermediaries. The other three parts of the marketing mix are product, pricing, and promotion.
Integrated marketing	Integrated Marketing Communication is the application of consistent brand messaging across both traditional and non-traditional marketing channels and using different promotional methods to reinforce each other.
Digital marketing	Digital marketing is marketing that makes use of electronic devices such as personal computers, smartphones, cellphones, tablets and game consoles to engage with stakeholders. Digital marketing applies technologies or platforms such as websites, e-mail, apps (classic and mobile) and social networks. Social Media Marketing is a component of digital marketing.
Delivery	Delivery is the process of transporting goods from a source location to a predefined destination. There are different delivery types. Cargo (physical goods) are primarily delivered via roads and railroads on land, shipping lanes on the sea and airline networks in the air.
Flow	Flow is middleware software, which allows data integration specialists to connect disparate systems, whether they are on-premise, hosted or in the cloud; transforming and restructuring data as required between environments. Flow functionality can be utilised for data integration projects, EDI and data conversion activities. Flow has been created by Flow Software Ltd in NZ and is available through a variety of partner companies or directly from Flow Software in NZ and Australia.
Sales	A sale is the act of selling a product or service in return for money or other compensation. Signalling completion of the prospective stage, it is the beginning of an engagement between customer and vendor or the extension of that engagement. The seller or salesperson - the provider of the goods or services - completes a sale in response to an acquisition or to an appropriation or to a request.
Service	In economics, a service is an intangible commodity. That is, services are an example of intangible economic goods.

12. Designing and Managing Integrated Marketing Channels

CHAPTER HIGHLIGHTS & NOTES: KEY TERMS, PEOPLE, PLACES, CONCEPTS

Direct marketing	Direct marketing is a channel-agnostic form of advertising which allows businesses and nonprofit organizations to communicate straight to the customer, with advertising techniques that can include cell phone text messaging, email, interactive consumer websites, online display ads, database marketing, fliers, catalog distribution, promotional letters, targeted television commercials, response-generating newspaper/magazine advertisements, and outdoor advertising. Amongst its practitioners, it is also referred to as Direct Response. Direct marketing messages emphasize a focus on the customer, data, and accountability.
Customer	A customer is the recipient of a good, service, product, or idea, obtained from a seller, vendor, or supplier for a monetary or other valuable consideration. Customers are generally categorized into two types:•An intermediate customer or trade customer who is a dealer that purchases goods for re-sale.•An ultimate customer who does not in turn re-sell the things bought but either passes them to the consumer or actually is the consumer. A customer may or may not also be a consumer, but the two notions are distinct, even though the terms are commonly confused. A customer purchases goods; a consumer uses them.
Social marketing	Social marketing seeks to develop and integrate marketing concepts with other approaches to influence behaviors that benefit individuals and communities for the greater social good. It seeks to integrate research, best practice, theory, audience and partnership insight, to inform the delivery of competition sensitive and segmented social change programs that are effective, efficient, equitable and sustainable. Although 'social marketing' is sometimes seen only as using standard commercial marketing practices to achieve non-commercial goals, this is an oversimplification.
Need	A need is something that is necessary for organisms to live a healthy life. Needs are distinguished from wants because a deficiency would cause a clear negative outcome, such as dysfunction or death. Needs can be objective and physical, such as food, or they can be subjective and psychological, such as the need for self-esteem.
QR code	QR code is the trademark for a type of matrix barcode (or two-dimensional barcode) first designed for the automotive industry in Japan. A barcode is a machine-readable optical label that contains information about the item to which it is attached. A QR code uses four standardized encoding modes (numeric, alphanumeric, byte / binary, and kanji) to efficiently store data; extensions may also be used.
Showrooming	Showrooming is the practice of examining merchandise in a traditional brick and mortar retail store, and then buying it online at a lower price. Online stores often offer lower prices than their brick and mortar counterparts, because they do not have the same overhead cost.

12. Designing and Managing Integrated Marketing Channels

CHAPTER HIGHLIGHTS & NOTES: KEY TERMS, PEOPLE, PLACES, CONCEPTS

Agent	In economics, an agent is an actor and decision maker in a model. Typically, every agent makes decisions by solving a well- or ill-defined optimization/choice problem. For example, buyers and sellers are two common types of agents in partial equilibrium models of a single market.
Interactive marketing	Interactive Marketing refers to the evolving trend in marketing whereby marketing has moved from a transaction-based effort to a conversation. John Deighton argued that interactive marketing features "the ability to address an individual and the ability to gather and remember the response of that individual" leading to "the ability to address the individual once more in a way that takes into account his or her unique response"(Deighton 1996). Interactive marketing is not synonymous with online marketing, although interactive marketing processes are facilitated by internet technology.
Merchant	A merchant is a businessperson who trades in commodities produced by others, in order to earn a profit. The status of the merchant has varied during different periods of history and amongst different societies. Merchants have often been the subject of works of art.
Horizontal marketing system	A horizontal marketing system is a distribution channel arrangement whereby two or more organizations at the same level join together for marketing purposes to capitalize on a new opportunity. For example: a bank and a supermarket agree to have the bank's ATMs located at the supermarket's locations, two manufacturers combining to achieve economies of scale, otherwise not possible with each acting alone, in meeting the needs and demands of a very large retailer, or two wholesalers joining together to serve a particular region at a certain time of year. According to businessdictionary.com, Horizontal Marketing System is a merger of firms on the same level in order to pursue marketing opportunities.
Consumer	A consumer is a person or group of people, such as a household, who are the final users of products or services. The consumer's use is final in the sense that the product is usually not improved by the use.
Customer service	Customer service is the provision of service to customers before, during and after a purchase. According to Turban et al. (2002), 'Customer service is a series of activities designed to enhance the level of customer satisfaction - that is, the feeling that a product or service has met the customer expectation.' The importance of customer service may vary by product or service, industry and customer. The perception of success of such interactions will be dependent on employees 'who can adjust themselves to the personality of the guest,' according to Micah Solomon.
Product	In marketing, a product is anything that can be offered to a market that might satisfy a want or need. In retailing, products are called merchandise.

12. Designing and Managing Integrated Marketing Channels

CHAPTER HIGHLIGHTS & NOTES: KEY TERMS, PEOPLE, PLACES, CONCEPTS

Big data	Big data is a blanket term for any collection of data sets so large and complex that it becomes difficult to process using on-hand database management tools or traditional data processing applications. The challenges include capture, curation, storage, search, sharing, transfer, analysis and visualization. The trend to larger data sets is due to the additional information derivable from analysis of a single large set of related data, as compared to separate smaller sets with the same total amount of data, allowing correlations to be found to 'spot business trends, determine quality of research, prevent diseases, link legal citations, combat crime, and determine real-time roadway traffic conditions.' Scientists regularly encounter limitations due to large data sets in many areas, including meteorology, genomics, connectomics, complex physics simulations, and biological and environmental research.
Channel conflict	Channel conflict occurs when manufacturers disintermediate their channel partners, such as distributors, retailers, dealers, and sales representatives, by selling their products directly to consumers through general marketing methods and/or over the Internet. Some manufacturers want to capture online markets for their brands but do not want to create conflicts with their other distribution channels. The Census Bureau of the U.S. Department of Commerce reported that online sales in 2005 grew 24.6 percent over 2004 to reach $86.3 billion dollars.
Advertising	Advertising or advertizing in business is a form of marketing communication used to encourage, persuade, or manipulate an audience to take or continue to take some action. Most commonly, the desired result is to drive consumer behavior with respect to a commercial offering, although political and ideological advertising is also common. This type of work belongs to a category called affective labor.
Promotion	Promotion is one of the market mix elements or features, and a term used frequently in marketing. The marketing mix includes the four P's: price, product, promotion, and place. Promotion refers to raising customer awareness of a product or brand, generating sales, and creating brand loyalty.
Shopping	A retailer or shop is a business that presents a selection of goods or services and offers to sell them to customers for money or other goods. Shopping is an activity in which a customer browses the available goods or services presented by one or more retailers with the intent to purchase a suitable selection of them. In some contexts it may be considered a leisure activity as well as an economic one.
Cannibalization	In marketing strategy, cannibalization refers to a reduction in sales volume, sales revenue, or market share of one product as a result of the introduction of a new product by the same producer.

12. Designing and Managing Integrated Marketing Channels

CHAPTER HIGHLIGHTS & NOTES: KEY TERMS, PEOPLE, PLACES, CONCEPTS

	While this may seem inherently negative, in the context of a carefully planned strategy, it can be effective, by ultimately growing the market, or better meeting consumer demands. Cannibalization is a key consideration in product portfolio analysis.
Co-optation	Co-option (also co-optation, sometimes spelled coöption or coöptation) has two common meanings:•the process of adding members to an elected or appointed group at the discretion of members of the body in order to fill vacancies, or to appoint additional members if permitted by the group's Constitution or rules.•the process by which a group subsumes or assimilates a smaller or weaker group with related interests; or, similarly, the process by which one group gains converts from another group by attempting to replicate the aspects that they find appealing without adopting the full program or ideals.
Exclusive dealing	In competition law, exclusive dealing refers to an arrangement whereby a retailer or wholesaler is 'tied' to purchase from a supplier on the understanding that no other distributor will be appointed or receive supplies in a given area. When the sales outlets are owned by the supplier, exclusive dealing is because of vertical integration, where the outlets are independent exclusive dealing is illegal (in the US) due to the Restrictive Trade Practices Act, however, if it is registered and approved it is allowed. Exclusive dealing can be a barrier to entry.
Mediation	Mediation, as used in law, is a form of alternative dispute resolution, a way of resolving disputes between two or more parties with concrete effects. Typically, a third party, the mediator, assists the parties to negotiate a settlement. Disputants may mediate disputes in a variety of domains, such as commercial, legal, diplomatic, workplace, community and family matters.
Perception	Perception is the organization, identification, and interpretation of sensory information in order to represent and understand the environment. All perception involves signals in the nervous system, which in turn result from physical or chemical stimulation of the sense organs. For example, vision involves light striking the retina of the eye, smell is mediated by odor molecules, and hearing involves pressure waves.

12. Designing and Managing Integrated Marketing Channels

CHAPTER QUIZ: KEY TERMS, PEOPLE, PLACES, CONCEPTS

1. Product _____ is one of the four elements of the marketing mix. _____ is the process of making a product or service available for use or consumption by a consumer or business user, using direct means, or using indirect means with intermediaries.

   The other three parts of the marketing mix are product, pricing, and promotion.

   a. Back to school
   b. Backward invention
   c. Bass diffusion model
   d. Distribution

2. In marketing strategy, _____ refers to a reduction in sales volume, sales revenue, or market share of one product as a result of the introduction of a new product by the same producer.

   While this may seem inherently negative, in the context of a carefully planned strategy, it can be effective, by ultimately growing the market, or better meeting consumer demands. _____ is a key consideration in product portfolio analysis.

   a. Back to school
   b. Backward invention
   c. Cannibalization
   d. Bayesian inference in marketing

3. In economics, an _____ is an actor and decision maker in a model. Typically, every _____ makes decisions by solving a well- or ill-defined optimization/choice problem.

   For example, buyers and sellers are two common types of _____s in partial equilibrium models of a single market.

   a. Total Immersion
   b. Barker channel
   c. Agent
   d. Bespoke Music

4. . Electronic commerce, commonly known as _____ or eCommerce, is trading in products or services using computer networks, such as the Internet. Electronic commerce draws on technologies such as mobile commerce, electronic funds transfer, supply chain management, Internet marketing, online transaction processing, electronic data interchange (EDI), inventory management systems, and automated data collection systems. Modern electronic commerce typically uses the World Wide Web for at least one part of the transaction's life cycle, although it may also use other technologies such as e-mail, mobile devices, social media, and telephones.

   a. Total Immersion
   b. Bespoke Music
   c. Barker channel

12. Designing and Managing Integrated Marketing Channels

CHAPTER QUIZ: KEY TERMS, PEOPLE, PLACES, CONCEPTS

5. _____ is marketing that makes use of electronic devices such as personal computers, smartphones, cellphones, tablets and game consoles to engage with stakeholders. _____ applies technologies or platforms such as websites, e-mail, apps (classic and mobile) and social networks. Social Media Marketing is a component of _____.

   a. Brand infiltration
   b. 140 Proof
   c. Barker channel
   d. Digital marketing

ANSWER KEY
12. Designing and Managing Integrated Marketing Channels

1. d
2. c
3. c
4. d
5. d

You can take the complete Chapter Practice Test

for 12. Designing and Managing Integrated Marketing Channels
on all key terms, persons, places, and concepts.

Online 99 Cents

http://www.JustTheFacts101.com

Use www.JustTheFacts101.com for all your study needs including Facts101's online interactive problem solving labs in chemistry, statistics, mathematics, and more.

13. Managing Retailing, Wholesaling, and Logistics

CHAPTER OUTLINE: KEY TERMS, PEOPLE, PLACES, CONCEPTS

_____ Service level

_____ Big data

_____ Direct marketing

_____ Direct selling

_____ Nonprofit

_____ E-commerce

_____ Shopping

_____ Mission statement

_____ Shopper marketing

_____ Label

_____ Multichannel marketing

_____ Service

_____ Pricing strategies

_____ Procurement

_____ Interactive marketing

_____ Research and development

_____ Sales

_____ Supply chain

_____ Supply chain management

_____ Inventory

_____ Market

13. Managing Retailing, Wholesaling, and Logistics
CHAPTER OUTLINE: KEY TERMS, PEOPLE, PLACES, CONCEPTS

	Order processing
	Cost

CHAPTER HIGHLIGHTS & NOTES: KEY TERMS, PEOPLE, PLACES, CONCEPTS

Service level	Service level measures the performance of a system. Certain goals are defined and the service level gives the percentage to which those goals should be achieved. Fill rate is different from service level.
Big data	Big data is a blanket term for any collection of data sets so large and complex that it becomes difficult to process using on-hand database management tools or traditional data processing applications.

The challenges include capture, curation, storage, search, sharing, transfer, analysis and visualization. The trend to larger data sets is due to the additional information derivable from analysis of a single large set of related data, as compared to separate smaller sets with the same total amount of data, allowing correlations to be found to 'spot business trends, determine quality of research, prevent diseases, link legal citations, combat crime, and determine real-time roadway traffic conditions.'

Scientists regularly encounter limitations due to large data sets in many areas, including meteorology, genomics, connectomics, complex physics simulations, and biological and environmental research. |
| Direct marketing | Direct marketing is a channel-agnostic form of advertising which allows businesses and nonprofit organizations to communicate straight to the customer, with advertising techniques that can include cell phone text messaging, email, interactive consumer websites, online display ads, database marketing, fliers, catalog distribution, promotional letters, targeted television commercials, response-generating newspaper/magazine advertisements, and outdoor advertising. Amongst its practitioners, it is also referred to as Direct Response.

Direct marketing messages emphasize a focus on the customer, data, and accountability. |
| Direct selling | Direct selling is the marketing and selling of products directly to consumers away from a fixed retail location. Peddling is the oldest form of direct selling. |

13. Managing Retailing, Wholesaling, and Logistics

CHAPTER HIGHLIGHTS & NOTES: KEY TERMS, PEOPLE, PLACES, CONCEPTS

Nonprofit	A nonprofit organization is an organization that uses surplus revenues to achieve its goals rather than distributing them as profit or dividends. While not-for-profit organizations are permitted to generate surplus revenues, they must be retained by the organization for its self-preservation, expansion, or plans. NPOs have controlling members or a board of directors.
E-commerce	Electronic commerce, commonly known as E-commerce or eCommerce, is trading in products or services using computer networks, such as the Internet. Electronic commerce draws on technologies such as mobile commerce, electronic funds transfer, supply chain management, Internet marketing, online transaction processing, electronic data interchange (EDI), inventory management systems, and automated data collection systems. Modern electronic commerce typically uses the World Wide Web for at least one part of the transaction's life cycle, although it may also use other technologies such as e-mail, mobile devices, social media, and telephones.
Shopping	A retailer or shop is a business that presents a selection of goods or services and offers to sell them to customers for money or other goods. Shopping is an activity in which a customer browses the available goods or services presented by one or more retailers with the intent to purchase a suitable selection of them. In some contexts it may be considered a leisure activity as well as an economic one.
Mission statement	A mission statement is a statement of the purpose of a company, organization or person, its reason for existing. The mission statement should guide the actions of the organization, spell out its overall goal, provide a path, and guide decision-making. It provides 'the framework or context within which the company's strategies are formulated.' It's like a goal for what the company wants to do for the world.
Shopper marketing	Shopper marketing is 'understanding how one's target consumers behave as shoppers, in different channels and formats, and leveraging this intelligence to the benefit of all stakeholders, defined as brands, consumers, retailers and shoppers.' According to Chris Hoyt 'Shopper marketing [is] brand marketing in retail environment.' Since it includes category management, displays, sales, packaging, promotion, research and marketing 'Shopper marketing is the elephant in the room that nobody sees the same way.' ([Shopper Marketing book], Kogan Page 2009) Shopper marketing is not limited to in-store marketing activities, a common and highly inaccurate assumption that impairs the spread of any industry definition. Shopper marketing must be part of an overall integrated marketing approach that considers the opportunities to drive consumption and identifies the shopper that would need to purchase a brand to enable that consumption.

13. Managing Retailing, Wholesaling, and Logistics

CHAPTER HIGHLIGHTS & NOTES: KEY TERMS, PEOPLE, PLACES, CONCEPTS

Label	A label is a piece of paper, polymer, cloth, metal, or other material affixed to a container or product, on which is printed information about the product
	Labels have many uses including providing information on a product's origin, use, shelf-life and disposal, some or all of which may be governed by legislation such as that for food in the UK. Methods of production and attachment to packaging are many and various and may also be subject to internationally recognised standards.
Multichannel marketing	Multichannel marketing is marketing using many different marketing channels to reach a customer. In this sense, a channel might be a retail store, a web site, a mail order catalogue, or direct personal communications by letter, email or text message. The objective of the companies doing the marketing is to make it easy for a consumer to buy from them in whatever way is most appropriate.
Service	In economics, a service is an intangible commodity. That is, services are an example of intangible economic goods.
	Service provision is often an economic activity where the buyer does not generally, except by exclusive contract, obtain exclusive ownership of the thing purchased.
Pricing strategies	A business can use a variety of pricing strategies when selling a product or service. The Price can be set to maximize profitability for each unit sold or from the market overall. It can be used to defend an existing market from new entrants, to increase market share within a market or to enter a new market.
Procurement	Procurement is the acquisition of goods, services or works from an external source. It is favourable that the goods, services or works are appropriate and that they are procured at the best possible cost to meet the needs of the acquirer in terms of quality and quantity, time, and location. Corporations and public bodies often define processes intended to promote fair and open competition for their business while minimizing exposure to fraud and collusion.
Interactive marketing	Interactive Marketing refers to the evolving trend in marketing whereby marketing has moved from a transaction-based effort to a conversation. John Deighton argued that interactive marketing features "the ability to address an individual and the ability to gather and remember the response of that individual" leading to "the ability to address the individual once more in a way that takes into account his or her unique response"(Deighton 1996). Interactive marketing is not synonymous with online marketing, although interactive marketing processes are facilitated by internet technology.
Research and development	The research and development is a specific group of activities within a business. The activities that are classified as R&D differ from company to company, but there are two primary models.

13. Managing Retailing, Wholesaling, and Logistics

CHAPTER HIGHLIGHTS & NOTES: KEY TERMS, PEOPLE, PLACES, CONCEPTS

Sales	A sale is the act of selling a product or service in return for money or other compensation. Signalling completion of the prospective stage, it is the beginning of an engagement between customer and vendor or the extension of that engagement. The seller or salesperson - the provider of the goods or services - completes a sale in response to an acquisition or to an appropriation or to a request.
Supply chain	A supply chain is a system of organizations, people, activities, information, and resources involved in moving a product or service from supplier to customer. Supply chain activities transform natural resources, raw materials, and components into a finished product that is delivered to the end customer. In sophisticated supply chain systems, used products may re-enter the supply chain at any point where residual value is recyclable.
Supply chain management	Supply chain management is the management of the flow of goods. It includes the movement and storage of raw materials, work-in-process inventory, and finished goods from point of origin to point of consumption. Interconnected or interlinked networks, channels and node businesses are involved in the provision of products and services required by end customers in a supply chain.
Inventory	Inventory or stock refers to the goods and materials that a business holds for the ultimate purpose of resale . Inventory management is a science primarily about specifying the shape and percentage of stocked goods. It is required at different locations within a facility or within many locations of a supply network to precede the regular and planned course of production and stock of materials.
Market	A market is one of the many varieties of systems, institutions, procedures, social relations and infrastructures whereby parties engage in exchange. While parties may exchange goods and services by barter, most markets rely on sellers offering their goods or services (including labor) in exchange for money from buyers. It can be said that a market is the process by which the prices of goods and services are established.
Order processing	Order Processing Order processing is a key element of Order fulfillment. Order processing operations or facilities are commonly called 'distribution centers'. 'Order processing' is the term generally used to describe the process or the work flow associated with the picking, packing and delivery of the packed item(s) to a shipping carrier.
Cost	In production, research, retail, and accounting, a cost is the value of money that has been used up to produce something, and hence is not available for use anymore. In business, the cost may be one of acquisition, in which case the amount of money expended to acquire it is counted as cost. In this case, money is the input that is gone in order to acquire the thing.

13. Managing Retailing, Wholesaling, and Logistics

CHAPTER QUIZ: KEY TERMS, PEOPLE, PLACES, CONCEPTS

1. The _____ is a specific group of activities within a business. The activities that are classified as R&D differ from company to company, but there are two primary models. In one model, the primary function of an R&D group is to develop new products; in the other model, the primary function of an R&D group is to discover and create new knowledge about scientific and technological topics for the purpose of uncovering and enabling development of valuable new products, processes, and services.

   a. Big Data Partnership
   b. CloverETL
   c. Research and development
   d. Continuuity

2. _____ is a channel-agnostic form of advertising which allows businesses and nonprofit organizations to communicate straight to the customer, with advertising techniques that can include cell phone text messaging, email, interactive consumer websites, online display ads, database marketing, fliers, catalog distribution, promotional letters, targeted television commercials, response-generating newspaper/magazine advertisements, and outdoor advertising. Amongst its practitioners, it is also referred to as Direct Response.

   _____ messages emphasize a focus on the customer, data, and accountability.

   a. Berlin promotion agency
   b. Boardroom, Inc.
   c. Boiler room
   d. Direct marketing

3. _____ is 'understanding how one's target consumers behave as shoppers, in different channels and formats, and leveraging this intelligence to the benefit of all stakeholders, defined as brands, consumers, retailers and shoppers.'

   According to Chris Hoyt '_____ [is] brand marketing in retail environment.' Since it includes category management, displays, sales, packaging, promotion, research and marketing '_____ is the elephant in the room that nobody sees the same way.' ([_____ book], Kogan Page 2009)

   _____ is not limited to in-store marketing activities, a common and highly inaccurate assumption that impairs the spread of any industry definition. _____ must be part of an overall integrated marketing approach that considers the opportunities to drive consumption and identifies the shopper that would need to purchase a brand to enable that consumption. These shoppers need to be understood in terms of how well they interpret the needs of the consumer, what their own needs as a shopper are, where they are likely to shop, in which stores they can be influenced in, and what in-store activity influences them.

   a. Business model
   b. Cause marketing
   c. Close Range Marketing
   d. Shopper marketing

13. Managing Retailing, Wholesaling, and Logistics

CHAPTER QUIZ: KEY TERMS, PEOPLE, PLACES, CONCEPTS

4. _____ is the marketing and selling of products directly to consumers away from a fixed retail location. Peddling is the oldest form of _____. Modern _____ includes sales made through the party plan, one-on-one demonstrations, and other personal contact arrangements as well as internet sales.

   a. Direct selling
   b. Barker channel
   c. 140 Proof
   d. Bespoke Music

5. _____ measures the performance of a system. Certain goals are defined and the _____ gives the percentage to which those goals should be achieved. Fill rate is different from _____.

   a. Service level
   b. Balance of contract
   c. Bridgewater House, Manchester
   d. Bullwhip effect

ANSWER KEY
13. Managing Retailing, Wholesaling, and Logistics

1. c
2. d
3. d
4. a
5. a

You can take the complete Chapter Practice Test

for 13. Managing Retailing, Wholesaling, and Logistics
on all key terms, persons, places, and concepts.

Online 99 Cents

http://www.JustTheFacts101.com

Use www.JustTheFacts101.com for all your study needs

including Facts101's online interactive problem solving labs in

chemistry, statistics, mathematics, and more.

14. Designing and Managing Integrated Marketing Communications

CHAPTER OUTLINE: KEY TERMS, PEOPLE, PLACES, CONCEPTS

- Advertising
- Big data
- Brand
- Marketing communications
- Mass marketing
- Sales promotion
- Brand equity
- Sales
- Database marketing
- Direct marketing
- Mobile marketing
- Public relations
- Publicity
- Social marketing
- Event
- Marketing
- Public
- Social media
- Lead time
- Mission statement
- Target audience

14. Designing and Managing Integrated Marketing Communications
CHAPTER OUTLINE: KEY TERMS, PEOPLE, PLACES, CONCEPTS

	Permission marketing
	Viral video
	Database
	Marketing mix
	Integrated marketing
	Marketing channel
	Marketing strategy

CHAPTER HIGHLIGHTS & NOTES: KEY TERMS, PEOPLE, PLACES, CONCEPTS

Advertising	Advertising or advertizing in business is a form of marketing communication used to encourage, persuade, or manipulate an audience to take or continue to take some action. Most commonly, the desired result is to drive consumer behavior with respect to a commercial offering, although political and ideological advertising is also common. This type of work belongs to a category called affective labor.
Big data	Big data is a blanket term for any collection of data sets so large and complex that it becomes difficult to process using on-hand database management tools or traditional data processing applications. The challenges include capture, curation, storage, search, sharing, transfer, analysis and visualization. The trend to larger data sets is due to the additional information derivable from analysis of a single large set of related data, as compared to separate smaller sets with the same total amount of data, allowing correlations to be found to 'spot business trends, determine quality of research, prevent diseases, link legal citations, combat crime, and determine real-time roadway traffic conditions.' Scientists regularly encounter limitations due to large data sets in many areas, including meteorology, genomics, connectomics, complex physics simulations, and biological and environmental research.

14. Designing and Managing Integrated Marketing Communications

CHAPTER HIGHLIGHTS & NOTES: KEY TERMS, PEOPLE, PLACES, CONCEPTS

Brand	Brand is the 'name, term, design, symbol, or any other feature that identifies one seller's product distinct from those of other sellers.' Brands are used in business, marketing, and advertising. Initially, livestock branding was adopted to differentiate one person's cattle from another's by means of a distinctive symbol burned into the animal's skin with a hot branding iron. A modern example of a brand is Coca-Cola which belongs to the Coca-Cola Company.
Marketing communications	Marketing communications are messages and related media used to communicate with a market. Marketing communications is the 'promotion' part of the 'marketing mix' or the 'four Ps': price, place, promotion, and product. It can also refer to the strategy used by a company or individual to reach their target market through various types of communication.
Mass marketing	Mass marketing is a market coverage strategy in which a firm decides to ignore market segment differences and appeal the whole market with one offer or one strategy. The idea is to broadcast a message that will reach the largest number of people possible. Traditionally mass marketing has focused on radio, television and newspapers as the media used to reach this broad audience.
Sales promotion	Sales promotion is one of the five aspects of the promotional mix. (The other 4 parts of the promotional mix are advertising, personal selling, direct marketing and publicity/public relations. Media and non-media marketing communication are employed for a pre-determined, limited time to increase consumer demand, stimulate market demand or improve product availability.
Brand equity	Brand equity is a phrase used in the marketing industry which describes the value of having a well-known brand name, based on the idea that the owner of a well-known brand name can generate more money from products with that brand name than from products with a less well known name, as consumers believe that a product with a well-known name is better than products with less well-known names. Some marketing researchers have concluded that brands are one of the most valuable assets a company has, as brand equity is one of the factors which can increase the financial value of a brand to the brand owner, although not the only one. Elements that can be included in the valuation of brand equity include (but not limited to): changing market share, profit margins, consumer recognition of logos and other visual elements, brand language associations made by consumers, consumers' perceptions of quality and other relevant brand values.
Sales	A sale is the act of selling a product or service in return for money or other compensation. Signalling completion of the prospective stage, it is the beginning of an engagement between customer and vendor or the extension of that engagement. The seller or salesperson - the provider of the goods or services - completes a sale in response to an acquisition or to an appropriation or to a request.

14. Designing and Managing Integrated Marketing Communications

CHAPTER HIGHLIGHTS & NOTES: KEY TERMS, PEOPLE, PLACES, CONCEPTS

Database marketing	Database marketing is a form of direct marketing using databases of customers or potential customers to generate personalized communications in order to promote a product or service for marketing purposes. The method of communication can be any addressable medium, as in direct marketing. The distinction between direct and database marketing stems primarily from the attention paid to the analysis of data.
Direct marketing	Direct marketing is a channel-agnostic form of advertising which allows businesses and nonprofit organizations to communicate straight to the customer, with advertising techniques that can include cell phone text messaging, email, interactive consumer websites, online display ads, database marketing, fliers, catalog distribution, promotional letters, targeted television commercials, response-generating newspaper/magazine advertisements, and outdoor advertising. Amongst its practitioners, it is also referred to as Direct Response. Direct marketing messages emphasize a focus on the customer, data, and accountability.
Mobile marketing	Mobile marketing is marketing on or with a mobile device, such as a smart phone. Mobile marketing can provide customers with time and location sensitive, personalized information that promotes goods, services and ideas. In a more theoretical manner, academic Andreas Kaplan defines mobile marketing as 'any marketing activity conducted through a ubiquitous network to which consumers are constantly connected using a personal mobile device'.
Public relations	Public relations is the practice of managing the spread of information between an individual or an organization and the public. Public relations may include an organization or individual gaining exposure to their audiences using topics of public interest and news items that do not require direct payment. The aim of public relations by a company often is to persuade the public, investors, partners, employees, and other stakeholders to maintain a certain point of view about it, its leadership, products, or of political decisions.
Publicity	Publicity is the movement of information with the effect of increasing public awareness of a subject. The subjects of publicity include people (for example, politicians and performing artists), goods and services, organizations of all kinds, and works of art or entertainment. Publicity is gaining public visibility or awareness for a product, service or your company via the media.
Social marketing	Social marketing seeks to develop and integrate marketing concepts with other approaches to influence behaviors that benefit individuals and communities for the greater social good. It seeks to integrate research, best practice, theory, audience and partnership insight, to inform the delivery of competition sensitive and segmented social change programs that are effective, efficient, equitable and sustainable.

14. Designing and Managing Integrated Marketing Communications

CHAPTER HIGHLIGHTS & NOTES: KEY TERMS, PEOPLE, PLACES, CONCEPTS

Event	In computer science, an event is a type of synchronization mechanism that is used to indicate to waiting processes when a particular condition has become true. An event is an abstract data type with a boolean state and the following operations:•wait - when executed, causes the executing process to suspend until the event's state is set to true. If the state is already set to true has no effect.•set - sets the event's state to true, release all waiting processes.•clear - sets the event's state to false. Different implementations of events may provide different subsets of these possible operations; for example, the implementation provided by Microsoft Windows provides the operations wait (WaitForObject and related functions), set (SetEvent), and clear (ResetEvent).
Marketing	Marketing is the process of communicating the value of a product or service to customers, for the purpose of selling that product or service. Marketing can be looked at as an organizational function and a set of processes for creating, delivering and communicating value to customers, and customer relationship management that also benefits the organization. Marketing is the science of choosing target markets through market analysis and market segmentation, as well as understanding consumer behavior and providing superior customer value.
Public	In public relations and communication science, publics are groups of individual people, and the public is the totality of such groupings. This is a different concept to the sociological concept of the Öffentlichkeit or public sphere. The concept of a public has also been defined in political science, psychology, marketing, and advertising.
Social media	Social media is the social interaction among people in which they create, share or exchange information and ideas in virtual communities and networks. Andreas Kaplan and Michael Haenlein define social media as 'a group of Internet-based applications that build on the ideological and technological foundations of Web 2.0, and that allow the creation and exchange of user-generated content.' Furthermore, social media depend on mobile and web-based technologies to create highly interactive platforms through which individuals and communities share, co-create, discuss, and modify user-generated content. They introduce substantial and pervasive changes to communication between organizations, communities, and individuals.
Lead time	A lead time is the latency between the initiation and execution of a process. For example, the lead time between the placement of an order and delivery of a new car from a manufacturer may be anywhere from 2 weeks to 6 months. In industry, lead time reduction is an important part of lean manufacturing.
Mission statement	A mission statement is a statement of the purpose of a company, organization or person, its reason for existing.

14. Designing and Managing Integrated Marketing Communications

CHAPTER HIGHLIGHTS & NOTES: KEY TERMS, PEOPLE, PLACES, CONCEPTS

	The mission statement should guide the actions of the organization, spell out its overall goal, provide a path, and guide decision-making. It provides 'the framework or context within which the company's strategies are formulated.' It's like a goal for what the company wants to do for the world.
Target audience	In marketing and advertising, a target audience is a specific group of people within the target market at which a product or the marketing message of a product is aimed at. (Kotler 2000)... For example, if a company sells new diet programs for men with heart disease problems (target market) the communication may be aimed at the spouse (target audience) who takes care of the nutrition plan of her husband and child. A target audience can be formed of people of a certain age group, gender, marital status, etc., e.g. teenagers, females, single people, etc.
Permission marketing	Permission marketing is a term popularized by Seth Godin used in marketing in general and e-marketing specifically. The undesirable opposite of permission marketing is interruption marketing. Marketers obtain permission before advancing to the next step in the purchasing process.
Viral video	A viral video is a video that becomes popular through the process of Internet sharing, typically through video sharing websites, social media and email. Viral videos often contain humorous content and include televised comedy sketches, such as The Lonely Island's 'Lazy Sunday' and 'Dick in a Box', Numa Numa videos, The Evolution of Dance, Chocolate Rain on YouTube; and web-only productions such as I Got a Crush... on Obama. Some eyewitness events have also been caught on video and have 'gone viral' such as the Battle at Kruger.
Database	A database is an organized collection of data. The data are typically organized to model aspects of reality in a way that supports processes requiring this information. For example, modelling the availability of rooms in hotels in a way that supports finding a hotel with vacancies.
Marketing mix	The marketing mix is a business tool used in marketing and by marketers. The marketing mix is often crucial when determining a product or brand's offer, and is often associated with the four P's: price, product, promotion, and place. In service marketing, however, the four Ps are expanded to the seven P's or eight P's to address the different nature of services.
Integrated marketing	Integrated Marketing Communication is the application of consistent brand messaging across both traditional and non-traditional marketing channels and using different promotional methods to reinforce each other.
Marketing channel	A marketing channel is a set of practices or activities necessary to transfer the ownership of goods, and to move goods, from the point of production to the point of consumption and, as such, which consists of all the institutions and all the marketing activities in the marketing process.

14. Designing and Managing Integrated Marketing Communications

CHAPTER HIGHLIGHTS & NOTES: KEY TERMS, PEOPLE, PLACES, CONCEPTS

	A marketing channel is a useful tool for management. Roles of marketing channel in marketing strategies•Links producers to buyers.•Performs sales, advertising and promotion.•Influences the firm's pricing strategy.•Affecting product strategy through branding, policies, willingness to stock.•Customizes profits, install, maintain, offer credit, etc..
Marketing strategy	Marketing strategy is defined by David Aaker as a process that can allow an organization to concentrate its resources on the optimal opportunities with the goals of increasing sales and achieving a sustainable competitive advantage. Marketing strategy includes all basic and long-term activities in the field of marketing that deal with the analysis of the strategic initial situation of a company and the formulation, evaluation and selection of market-oriented strategies and therefore contribute to the goals of the company and its marketing objectives.

CHAPTER QUIZ: KEY TERMS, PEOPLE, PLACES, CONCEPTS

1. _____ is a phrase used in the marketing industry which describes the value of having a well-known brand name, based on the idea that the owner of a well-known brand name can generate more money from products with that brand name than from products with a less well known name, as consumers believe that a product with a well-known name is better than products with less well-known names.

    Some marketing researchers have concluded that brands are one of the most valuable assets a company has, as _____ is one of the factors which can increase the financial value of a brand to the brand owner, although not the only one. Elements that can be included in the valuation of _____ include (but not limited to): changing market share, profit margins, consumer recognition of logos and other visual elements, brand language associations made by consumers, consumers' perceptions of quality and other relevant brand values.

    a. Product management
    b. Product manager
    c. Big Data Partnership
    d. Brand equity

2. . _____ or advertizing in business is a form of marketing communication used to encourage, persuade, or manipulate an audience to take or continue to take some action. Most commonly, the desired result is to drive consumer behavior with respect to a commercial offering, although political and ideological _____ is also common. This type of work belongs to a category called affective labor.

    a. Big Data Partnership
    b. CloverETL

14. Designing and Managing Integrated Marketing Communications

CHAPTER QUIZ: KEY TERMS, PEOPLE, PLACES, CONCEPTS

   c. Advertising
   d. Continuuity

3. _____ is the 'name, term, design, symbol, or any other feature that identifies one seller's product distinct from those of other sellers.' _____s are used in business, marketing, and advertising. Initially, livestock branding was adopted to differentiate one person's cattle from another's by means of a distinctive symbol burned into the animal's skin with a hot branding iron. A modern example of a _____ is Coca-Cola which belongs to the Coca-Cola Company.

   a. Brand
   b. Backward invention
   c. Bass diffusion model
   d. Bayesian inference in marketing

4. _____ is one of the five aspects of the promotional mix. (The other 4 parts of the promotional mix are advertising, personal selling, direct marketing and publicity/public relations. Media and non-media marketing communication are employed for a pre-determined, limited time to increase consumer demand, stimulate market demand or improve product availability.

   a. Broadside
   b. Christine
   c. Sales promotion
   d. CollarCard

5. A _____ is the latency between the initiation and execution of a process. For example, the _____ between the placement of an order and delivery of a new car from a manufacturer may be anywhere from 2 weeks to 6 months. In industry, _____ reduction is an important part of lean manufacturing.

   a. Tulip mania
   b. Lead time
   c. Southwestern
   d. Corporate communication

ANSWER KEY
14. Designing and Managing Integrated Marketing Communications

1. d
2. c
3. a
4. c
5. b

You can take the complete Chapter Practice Test

for 14. Designing and Managing Integrated Marketing Communications
on all key terms, persons, places, and concepts.

Online 99 Cents

http://www.JustTheFacts101.com

Use www.JustTheFacts101.com for all your study needs

including Facts101's online interactive problem solving labs in

chemistry, statistics, mathematics, and more.

15. Managing Mass Communications: Advertising, Sales Promotions, Event

CHAPTER OUTLINE: KEY TERMS, PEOPLE, PLACES, CONCEPTS

	Mass marketing
	Advertising
	Advertising campaign
	Creative brief
	Informative advertising
	Reinforcement
	Media planner
	Alternative media
	Mobile marketing
	Reach
	Copy testing
	Flighting
	Search advertising
	Consumer cooperative
	Experiential marketing
	Sales promotion
	Share of voice
	Shareholder value
	Sales
	Trade promotion
	Coupon

15. Managing Mass Communications: Advertising, Sales Promotions, Events an ...

CHAPTER OUTLINE: KEY TERMS, PEOPLE, PLACES, CONCEPTS

_____	Lead time
_____	Marketing
_____	Public
_____	Public relations
_____	Publicity
_____	Chain store

CHAPTER HIGHLIGHTS & NOTES: KEY TERMS, PEOPLE, PLACES, CONCEPTS

Mass marketing	Mass marketing is a market coverage strategy in which a firm decides to ignore market segment differences and appeal the whole market with one offer or one strategy. The idea is to broadcast a message that will reach the largest number of people possible. Traditionally mass marketing has focused on radio, television and newspapers as the media used to reach this broad audience.
Advertising	Advertising or advertizing in business is a form of marketing communication used to encourage, persuade, or manipulate an audience to take or continue to take some action. Most commonly, the desired result is to drive consumer behavior with respect to a commercial offering, although political and ideological advertising is also common. This type of work belongs to a category called affective labor.
Advertising campaign	An advertising campaign is a series of advertisement messages that share a single idea and theme which make up an integrated marketing communication . Advertising campaigns appear in different media across a specific time frame of frequent flyers points. The critical part of making an advertising campaign is determining a campaign theme as it sets the tone for the individual advertisements and other forms of marketing communications that will be used.
Creative brief	A creative brief is a document used by creative professionals and agencies to develop creative deliverables: visual design, copy, advertising, web sites, etc. The document is usually developed by the requestor (in most cases a marketing team member) and approved by the creative team of designers, writers, and project managers.

15. Managing Mass Communications: Advertising, Sales Promotions, Events an ...

CHAPTER HIGHLIGHTS & NOTES: KEY TERMS, PEOPLE, PLACES, CONCEPTS

Informative advertising	Informative advertising is advertising that is carried out in an informative manner Also, informative ads tend to help generate a good reputation.
Reinforcement	In behavioral psychology, reinforcement is a consequence that will strengthen an organism's future behavior whenever that behavior is preceded by a specific antecedent stimulus. This strengthening effect may be measured as a higher frequency of behavior (e.g., pulling a lever more frequently), longer duration (e.g., pulling a lever for longer periods of time), greater magnitude (e.g., pulling a lever with greater force), or shorter latency (e.g., pulling a lever more quickly following the antecedent stimulus). Although in many cases a reinforcing stimulus is a rewarding stimulus which is 'valued' or 'liked' by the individual (e.g., money received from a slot machine, the taste of the treat, the euphoria produced by an addictive drug), this is not a requirement.
Media planner	Media planning is generally the task of a media agency and entails finding media platforms for a client's brand or product to use. The job of media planning is to determine the best combination of media to achieve the marketing campaign objectives. In the process of planning, the media planner needs to answer questions such as:•How many of the audience can be reached through the various media?•On which media (and ad vehicles) should the ads be placed?•How frequent should the ads be placed?•How much money should be spent in each medium? Choosing which media or type of advertising to use is sometimes tricky for small firms with limited budgets and know-how.
Alternative media	Alternative media are media which provide alternative information to the mainstream media in a given context, whether the mainstream media are commercial, publicly supported, or government-owned. Alternative media differ from mainstream media along one or more of the following dimensions: their content, aesthetic, modes of production, modes of distribution, and audience relations. Alternative media often aim to challenge existing powers, to represent marginalized groups, and to foster horizontal linkages among communities of interest.
Mobile marketing	Mobile marketing is marketing on or with a mobile device, such as a smart phone. Mobile marketing can provide customers with time and location sensitive, personalized information that promotes goods, services and ideas. In a more theoretical manner, academic Andreas Kaplan defines mobile marketing as 'any marketing activity conducted through a ubiquitous network to which consumers are constantly connected using a personal mobile device'.
Reach	In the application of statistics to advertising and media analysis, reach refers to the total number of different people or households exposed, at least once, to a medium during a given period.

15. Managing Mass Communications: Advertising, Sales Promotions, Events an ...

CHAPTER HIGHLIGHTS & NOTES: KEY TERMS, PEOPLE, PLACES, CONCEPTS

	Reach should not be confused with the number of people who will actually be exposed to and consume the advertising, though. It is just the number of people who are exposed to the medium and therefore have an opportunity to see or hear the ad or commercial.
Copy testing	Copy testing is a specialized field of marketing research that determines an ad's effectiveness based on consumer responses, feedback, and behavior. Also known as pre-testing, it covers all media channels including television, print, radio, internet, and social media.
Flighting	Flighting is an advertising term for a timing pattern in which commercials are scheduled to run during intervals that are separated by periods in which no advertising messages appear for the advertised item. Any period of time during which the messages are appearing is called a flight, and a period of message inactivity is usually called a 'hiatus'. The advantage of the flighting technique is that it allows an advertiser who does not have funds for running spots continuously to conserve money and maximize the impact of the commercials by airing them at key strategic times.
Search advertising	In Internet Marketing, Search Advertising is a method of placing online advertisements on Web pages that show results from search engine queries. Through the same search-engine advertising services, ads can also be placed on Web pages with other published. Search advertisements are targeted to match key search terms (called keywords) entered on search engines.
Consumer cooperative	Consumer cooperatives are enterprises owned by consumers and managed democratically which aim at fulfilling the needs and aspirations of their members. They operate within the market system, independently of the state, as a form of mutual aid, oriented toward service rather than pecuniary profit. Consumers' cooperatives often take the form of retail outlets owned and operated by their consumers, such as food co-ops.
Experiential marketing	Engagement marketing, sometimes called 'experiential marketing,' 'event marketing', 'on-ground marketing', 'live marketing' or 'participation marketing,' is a marketing strategy that directly engages consumers and invites and encourages consumers to participate in the evolution of a brand. Rather than looking at consumers as passive receivers of messages, engagement marketers believe that consumers should be actively involved in the production and co-creation of marketing programs, developing a relationship with the brand. Consumer Engagement is the ultimate point in which a brand and a consumer connect in order to offer a true experience related to the brand's core values.
Sales promotion	Sales promotion is one of the five aspects of the promotional mix. (The other 4 parts of the promotional mix are advertising, personal selling, direct marketing and publicity/public relations.

15. Managing Mass Communications: Advertising, Sales Promotions, Events an ...

CHAPTER HIGHLIGHTS & NOTES: KEY TERMS, PEOPLE, PLACES, CONCEPTS

Share of voice	Share of Voice in Online Advertising is an ad revenue model that focuses on weight or percentage among other advertisers. For example, if there are four advertisers on a website, each advertiser gets 25 percent of the advertising weight. This method ensures one ad will not be seen any more than the other three ads.
Shareholder value	Shareholder value is a business term, sometimes phrased as shareholder value maximization or as the shareholder value model, which implies that the ultimate measure of a company's success is the extent to which it enriches shareholders. It became popular during the 1980s, and is particularly associated with former CEO of General Electric, Jack Welch. The term used in several ways:•To refer to the market capitalization of a company (rarely used)•To refer to the concept that the primary goal for a company is to increase the wealth of its shareholders (owners) by paying dividends and/or causing the stock price to increase•To refer to the more specific concept that planned actions by management and the returns to shareholders should outperform certain bench-marks such as the cost of capital concept.
Sales	A sale is the act of selling a product or service in return for money or other compensation. Signalling completion of the prospective stage, it is the beginning of an engagement between customer and vendor or the extension of that engagement. The seller or salesperson - the provider of the goods or services - completes a sale in response to an acquisition or to an appropriation or to a request.
Trade promotion	In business and marketing, "trade" refers to the relationship between manufacturers and retailers. Trade Promotion refers to marketing activities that are executed in retail between these two partners. Trade Promotion is a marketing technique aimed at increasing demand for products in retail stores based on special pricing, display fixtures, demonstrations, value-added bonuses, no-obligation gifts, and more.
Coupon	In marketing, a coupon is a ticket or document that can be exchanged for a financial discount or rebate when purchasing a product. Customarily, coupons are issued by manufacturers of consumer packaged goods or by retailers, to be used in retail stores as a part of sales promotions. They are often widely distributed through mail, coupon envelopes, magazines, newspapers, the Internet (social media, email newsletter), directly from the retailer, and mobile devices such as cell phones.
Lead time	A lead time is the latency between the initiation and execution of a process. For example, the lead time between the placement of an order and delivery of a new car from a manufacturer may be anywhere from 2 weeks to 6 months. In industry, lead time reduction is an important part of lean manufacturing.

15. Managing Mass Communications: Advertising, Sales Promotions, Events an …

CHAPTER HIGHLIGHTS & NOTES: KEY TERMS, PEOPLE, PLACES, CONCEPTS

Marketing	Marketing is the process of communicating the value of a product or service to customers, for the purpose of selling that product or service. Marketing can be looked at as an organizational function and a set of processes for creating, delivering and communicating value to customers, and customer relationship management that also benefits the organization. Marketing is the science of choosing target markets through market analysis and market segmentation, as well as understanding consumer behavior and providing superior customer value.
Public	In public relations and communication science, publics are groups of individual people, and the public is the totality of such groupings. This is a different concept to the sociological concept of the Öffentlichkeit or public sphere. The concept of a public has also been defined in political science, psychology, marketing, and advertising.
Public relations	Public relations is the practice of managing the spread of information between an individual or an organization and the public. Public relations may include an organization or individual gaining exposure to their audiences using topics of public interest and news items that do not require direct payment. The aim of public relations by a company often is to persuade the public, investors, partners, employees, and other stakeholders to maintain a certain point of view about it, its leadership, products, or of political decisions.
Publicity	Publicity is the movement of information with the effect of increasing public awareness of a subject. The subjects of publicity include people (for example, politicians and performing artists), goods and services, organizations of all kinds, and works of art or entertainment. Publicity is gaining public visibility or awareness for a product, service or your company via the media.
Chain store	Chain stores are retail outlets that share a brand and central management, and usually have standardized business methods and practices. Before considered a chain, stores must meet a litmus test; it must have more than 10 units in 2 or more distinct geographies under the same brand and have a central headquarters, otherwise it offers franchise contracts or is publicly traded. These characteristics also apply to chain restaurants and some service-oriented chain businesses. In retail, dining, and many service categories, chain businesses have come to dominate the market in many parts of the world.

15. Managing Mass Communications: Advertising, Sales Promotions, Events an ...

CHAPTER QUIZ: KEY TERMS, PEOPLE, PLACES, CONCEPTS

1. _____ or advertizing in business is a form of marketing communication used to encourage, persuade, or manipulate an audience to take or continue to take some action. Most commonly, the desired result is to drive consumer behavior with respect to a commercial offering, although political and ideological _____ is also common. This type of work belongs to a category called affective labor.

   a. Big Data Partnership
   b. CloverETL
   c. Compuverde
   d. Advertising

2. _____ is the practice of managing the spread of information between an individual or an organization and the public. _____ may include an organization or individual gaining exposure to their audiences using topics of public interest and news items that do not require direct payment. The aim of _____ by a company often is to persuade the public, investors, partners, employees, and other stakeholders to maintain a certain point of view about it, its leadership, products, or of political decisions.

   a. Public relations
   b. Celestino Piatti
   c. Chalcography
   d. Chief creative officer

3. A _____ is a document used by creative professionals and agencies to develop creative deliverables: visual design, copy, advertising, web sites, etc. The document is usually developed by the requestor (in most cases a marketing team member) and approved by the creative team of designers, writers, and project managers. In some cases, the project's _____ may need creative director approval before work will commence.

   a. 140 Proof
   b. Creative brief
   c. Bespoke Music
   d. Bibliography of advertising

4. _____ is a specialized field of marketing research that determines an ad's effectiveness based on consumer responses, feedback, and behavior. Also known as pre-testing, it covers all media channels including television, print, radio, internet, and social media.

   a. 140 Proof
   b. Barker channel
   c. Copy testing
   d. Bibliography of advertising

5. . _____s are retail outlets that share a brand and central management, and usually have standardized business methods and practices.

15. Managing Mass Communications: Advertising, Sales Promotions, Events an ...

CHAPTER QUIZ: KEY TERMS, PEOPLE, PLACES, CONCEPTS

Before considered a chain, stores must meet a litmus test; it must have more than 10 units in 2 or more distinct geographies under the same brand and have a central headquarters, otherwise it offers franchise contracts or is publicly traded.These characteristics also apply to chain restaurants and some service-oriented chain businesses. In retail, dining, and many service categories, chain businesses have come to dominate the market in many parts of the world.

a. Best before
b. Chain store
c. Black Friday
d. Boutique

ANSWER KEY
15. Managing Mass Communications: Advertising, Sales Promotions, Events an ...

1. d
2. a
3. b
4. c
5. b

You can take the complete Chapter Practice Test

for 15. Managing Mass Communications: Advertising, Sales Promotions, Events an ...
on all key terms, persons, places, and concepts.

Online 99 Cents

http://www.JustTheFacts101.com

Use www.JustTheFacts101.com for all your study needs

including Facts101's online interactive problem solving labs in

chemistry, statistics, mathematics, and more.

16. Managing Digital Communications: Online, Social Media, and Mobile

CHAPTER OUTLINE: KEY TERMS, PEOPLE, PLACES, CONCEPTS

- _____ Marketing communications
- _____ Brand equity
- _____ Earned media
- _____ Social marketing
- _____ Search engine optimization
- _____ Social media
- _____ Blog
- _____ Social network
- _____ Viral marketing
- _____ Marketing
- _____ Word of mouth
- _____ Customer
- _____ Mobile marketing
- _____ Mass marketing
- _____ Mission statement
- _____ Advertising
- _____ Scope

16. Managing Digital Communications: Online, Social Media, and Mobile

CHAPTER HIGHLIGHTS & NOTES: KEY TERMS, PEOPLE, PLACES, CONCEPTS

Marketing communications	Marketing communications are messages and related media used to communicate with a market. Marketing communications is the 'promotion' part of the 'marketing mix' or the 'four Ps': price, place, promotion, and product. It can also refer to the strategy used by a company or individual to reach their target market through various types of communication.
Brand equity	Brand equity is a phrase used in the marketing industry which describes the value of having a well-known brand name, based on the idea that the owner of a well-known brand name can generate more money from products with that brand name than from products with a less well known name, as consumers believe that a product with a well-known name is better than products with less well-known names. Some marketing researchers have concluded that brands are one of the most valuable assets a company has, as brand equity is one of the factors which can increase the financial value of a brand to the brand owner, although not the only one. Elements that can be included in the valuation of brand equity include (but not limited to): changing market share, profit margins, consumer recognition of logos and other visual elements, brand language associations made by consumers, consumers' perceptions of quality and other relevant brand values.
Earned media	Earned media refers to publicity gained through promotional efforts other than advertising, as opposed to paid media, which refers to publicity gained through advertising.
Social marketing	Social marketing seeks to develop and integrate marketing concepts with other approaches to influence behaviors that benefit individuals and communities for the greater social good. It seeks to integrate research, best practice, theory, audience and partnership insight, to inform the delivery of competition sensitive and segmented social change programs that are effective, efficient, equitable and sustainable. Although 'social marketing' is sometimes seen only as using standard commercial marketing practices to achieve non-commercial goals, this is an oversimplification.
Search engine optimization	Search engine optimization is the process of affecting the visibility of a website or a web page in a search engine's 'natural' or un-paid ('organic') search results. In general, the earlier (or higher ranked on the search results page), and more frequently a site appears in the search results list, the more visitors it will receive from the search engine's users. Search engine optimization may target different kinds of search, including image search, local search, video search, academic search, news search and industry-specific vertical search engines.
Social media	Social media is the social interaction among people in which they create, share or exchange information and ideas in virtual communities and networks.

16. Managing Digital Communications: Online, Social Media, and Mobile

CHAPTER HIGHLIGHTS & NOTES: KEY TERMS, PEOPLE, PLACES, CONCEPTS

	Andreas Kaplan and Michael Haenlein define social media as 'a group of Internet-based applications that build on the ideological and technological foundations of Web 2.0, and that allow the creation and exchange of user-generated content.' Furthermore, social media depend on mobile and web-based technologies to create highly interactive platforms through which individuals and communities share, co-create, discuss, and modify user-generated content. They introduce substantial and pervasive changes to communication between organizations, communities, and individuals.
Blog	A blog is a discussion or informational site published on the World Wide Web and consisting of discrete entries typically displayed in reverse chronological order (the most recent post appears first). Until 2009 blogs were usually the work of a single individual, occasionally of a small group, and often covered a single subject. More recently 'multi-author blogs' (MABs) have developed, with posts written by large numbers of authors and professionally edited.
Social network	A social network is a social structure made up of a set of social actors and a set of the dyadic ties between these actors. The social network perspective provides a set of methods for analyzing the structure of whole social entities as well as a variety of theories explaining the patterns observed in these structures. The study of these structures uses social network analysis to identify local and global patterns, locate influential entities, and examine network dynamics.
Viral marketing	Viral marketing, viral advertising, or marketing buzz are buzzwords referring to marketing techniques that use pre-existing social networking services and other technologies to try to produce increases in brand awareness or to achieve other marketing objectives through self-replicating viral processes, analogous to the spread of viruses or computer viruses (cf. Internet memes and memetics). It can be delivered by word of mouth or enhanced by the network effects of the Internet and mobile networks.
Marketing	Marketing is the process of communicating the value of a product or service to customers, for the purpose of selling that product or service.
	Marketing can be looked at as an organizational function and a set of processes for creating, delivering and communicating value to customers, and customer relationship management that also benefits the organization. Marketing is the science of choosing target markets through market analysis and market segmentation, as well as understanding consumer behavior and providing superior customer value.
Word of mouth	Word of mouth, or viva voce, is the passing of information from person to person by oral communication, which could be as simple as telling someone the time of day. Storytelling is a common form of word-of-mouth communication where one person tells others a story about a real event or something made up. Oral tradition is cultural material and traditions transmitted by word of mouth through successive generations.

16. Managing Digital Communications: Online, Social Media, and Mobile

CHAPTER HIGHLIGHTS & NOTES: KEY TERMS, PEOPLE, PLACES, CONCEPTS

Customer	A customer is the recipient of a good, service, product, or idea, obtained from a seller, vendor, or supplier for a monetary or other valuable consideration. Customers are generally categorized into two types:•An intermediate customer or trade customer who is a dealer that purchases goods for re-sale.•An ultimate customer who does not in turn re-sell the things bought but either passes them to the consumer or actually is the consumer. A customer may or may not also be a consumer, but the two notions are distinct, even though the terms are commonly confused. A customer purchases goods; a consumer uses them.
Mobile marketing	Mobile marketing is marketing on or with a mobile device, such as a smart phone. Mobile marketing can provide customers with time and location sensitive, personalized information that promotes goods, services and ideas. In a more theoretical manner, academic Andreas Kaplan defines mobile marketing as 'any marketing activity conducted through a ubiquitous network to which consumers are constantly connected using a personal mobile device'.
Mass marketing	Mass marketing is a market coverage strategy in which a firm decides to ignore market segment differences and appeal the whole market with one offer or one strategy. The idea is to broadcast a message that will reach the largest number of people possible. Traditionally mass marketing has focused on radio, television and newspapers as the media used to reach this broad audience.
Mission statement	A mission statement is a statement of the purpose of a company, organization or person, its reason for existing. The mission statement should guide the actions of the organization, spell out its overall goal, provide a path, and guide decision-making. It provides 'the framework or context within which the company's strategies are formulated.' It's like a goal for what the company wants to do for the world.
Advertising	Advertising or advertizing in business is a form of marketing communication used to encourage, persuade, or manipulate an audience to take or continue to take some action. Most commonly, the desired result is to drive consumer behavior with respect to a commercial offering, although political and ideological advertising is also common. This type of work belongs to a category called affective labor.
Scope	In project management, the term scope has two distinct uses- Project Scope and Product Scope. Scope involves getting information required to start a project, and the features the product would have that would meet its stakeholders requirements. Project Scope'The work that needs to be accomplished to deliver a product, service, or result with the specified features and functions.'Product Scope'The features and functions that characterize a product, service, or result.'

16. Managing Digital Communications: Online, Social Media, and Mobile

CHAPTER QUIZ: KEY TERMS, PEOPLE, PLACES, CONCEPTS

1. _____ is the process of affecting the visibility of a website or a web page in a search engine's 'natural' or un-paid ('organic') search results. In general, the earlier (or higher ranked on the search results page), and more frequently a site appears in the search results list, the more visitors it will receive from the search engine's users. _____ may target different kinds of search, including image search, local search, video search, academic search, news search and industry-specific vertical search engines.

   a. Bounce rate
   b. Content farm
   c. Corporate blog
   d. Search engine optimization

2. In project management, the term _____ has two distinct uses- Project _____ and Product _____.

   _____ involves getting information required to start a project, and the features the product would have that would meet its stakeholders requirements. Project _____ 'The work that needs to be accomplished to deliver a product, service, or result with the specified features and functions.' Product _____ 'The features and functions that characterize a product, service, or result.'

   Notice that Project _____ is more work-oriented, while Product _____ is more oriented toward functional requirements.

   a. 10,000ft
   b. Basis of estimate
   c. Bid manager
   d. Scope

3. A _____ is a statement of the purpose of a company, organization or person, its reason for existing.

   The _____ should guide the actions of the organization, spell out its overall goal, provide a path, and guide decision-making. It provides 'the framework or context within which the company's strategies are formulated.' It's like a goal for what the company wants to do for the world.

   a. strategic planning
   b. Traffic manager
   c. Non-commercial
   d. Mission statement

4. . _____ are messages and related media used to communicate with a market. _____ is the 'promotion' part of the 'marketing mix' or the 'four Ps': price, place, promotion, and product. It can also refer to the strategy used by a company or individual to reach their target market through various types of communication.

   a. Back to school
   b. Marketing communications

16. Managing Digital Communications: Online, Social Media, and Mobile

CHAPTER QUIZ: KEY TERMS, PEOPLE, PLACES, CONCEPTS

   c. Bass diffusion model
   d. Bayesian inference in marketing

5. _____ is a phrase used in the marketing industry which describes the value of having a well-known brand name, based on the idea that the owner of a well-known brand name can generate more money from products with that brand name than from products with a less well known name, as consumers believe that a product with a well-known name is better than products with less well-known names.

   Some marketing researchers have concluded that brands are one of the most valuable assets a company has, as _____ is one of the factors which can increase the financial value of a brand to the brand owner, although not the only one. Elements that can be included in the valuation of _____ include (but not limited to): changing market share, profit margins, consumer recognition of logos and other visual elements, brand language associations made by consumers, consumers' perceptions of quality and other relevant brand values.

   a. Product management
   b. Brand equity
   c. Big Data Partnership
   d. CloverETL

ANSWER KEY
16. Managing Digital Communications: Online, Social Media, and Mobile

1. d
2. d
3. d
4. b
5. b

You can take the complete Chapter Practice Test

for 16. Managing Digital Communications: Online, Social Media, and Mobile
on all key terms, persons, places, and concepts.

Online 99 Cents

http://www.JustTheFacts101.com

Use www.JustTheFacts101.com for all your study needs including Facts101's online interactive problem solving labs in chemistry, statistics, mathematics, and more.

17. Managing Personal Communications: Direct and Database Marketing a

CHAPTER OUTLINE: KEY TERMS, PEOPLE, PLACES, CONCEPTS

- _____ Database marketing
- _____ Direct marketing
- _____ Mailing list
- _____ Marketing communications
- _____ Brand equity
- _____ Direct mail
- _____ National Do Not Call Registry
- _____ Telemarketing
- _____ Business-to-business
- _____ Service
- _____ Customer
- _____ Database
- _____ Infomercial
- _____ Home shopping
- _____ Marketing
- _____ Sales
- _____ Relationship marketing
- _____ Sales process
- _____ Marketing management
- _____ Account manager
- _____ Social marketing

17. Managing Personal Communications: Direct and Database Marketing and Pe ...
CHAPTER OUTLINE: KEY TERMS, PEOPLE, PLACES, CONCEPTS

	Social network
	Selling
	Feedback
	Performance

CHAPTER HIGHLIGHTS & NOTES: KEY TERMS, PEOPLE, PLACES, CONCEPTS

Database marketing	Database marketing is a form of direct marketing using databases of customers or potential customers to generate personalized communications in order to promote a product or service for marketing purposes. The method of communication can be any addressable medium, as in direct marketing. The distinction between direct and database marketing stems primarily from the attention paid to the analysis of data.
Direct marketing	Direct marketing is a channel-agnostic form of advertising which allows businesses and nonprofit organizations to communicate straight to the customer, with advertising techniques that can include cell phone text messaging, email, interactive consumer websites, online display ads, database marketing, fliers, catalog distribution, promotional letters, targeted television commercials, response-generating newspaper/magazine advertisements, and outdoor advertising. Amongst its practitioners, it is also referred to as Direct Response. Direct marketing messages emphasize a focus on the customer, data, and accountability.
Mailing list	A mailing list is a collection of names and addresses used by an individual or an organization to send material to multiple recipients. The term is often extended to include the people subscribed to such a list, so the group of subscribers is referred to as 'the mailing list', or simply 'the list'.
Marketing communications	Marketing communications are messages and related media used to communicate with a market. Marketing communications is the 'promotion' part of the 'marketing mix' or the 'four Ps': price, place, promotion, and product. It can also refer to the strategy used by a company or individual to reach their target market through various types of communication.

17. Managing Personal Communications: Direct and Database Marketing and Pe ...

CHAPTER HIGHLIGHTS & NOTES: KEY TERMS, PEOPLE, PLACES, CONCEPTS

Brand equity	Brand equity is a phrase used in the marketing industry which describes the value of having a well-known brand name, based on the idea that the owner of a well-known brand name can generate more money from products with that brand name than from products with a less well known name, as consumers believe that a product with a well-known name is better than products with less well-known names. Some marketing researchers have concluded that brands are one of the most valuable assets a company has, as brand equity is one of the factors which can increase the financial value of a brand to the brand owner, although not the only one. Elements that can be included in the valuation of brand equity include (but not limited to): changing market share, profit margins, consumer recognition of logos and other visual elements, brand language associations made by consumers, consumers' perceptions of quality and other relevant brand values.
Direct mail	Advertising mail, also known as direct mail, junk mail (occasionally, by its recipients), or admail, is the delivery of advertising material to recipients of postal mail. The delivery of advertising mail forms a large and growing service for many postal services, and direct-mail marketing forms a significant portion of the direct marketing industry. Some organizations attempt to help people opt out of receiving advertising mail, in many cases motivated by a concern over its negative environmental impact.
National Do Not Call Registry	The National Do Not Call Registry is intended to give U.S. consumers an opportunity to limit the telemarketing calls they receive. To register by telephone (US), consumers may call 1-888-382-1222; or they may register via the web at the DoNotCall.gov registration page. The registry was set to begin in 2003, but a court challenge delayed its implementation until 2004. The law provides exceptions to a blanket do-not-call ruling.
Telemarketing	Telemarketing is a method of direct marketing in which a salesperson solicits prospective customers to buy products or services, either over the phone or through a subsequent face to face or Web conferencing appointment scheduled during the call. Telemarketing can also include recorded sales pitches programmed to be played over the phone via automatic dialing.
Business-to-business	Business-to-business describes commerce transactions between businesses, such as between a manufacturer and a wholesaler, or between a wholesaler and a retailer. Contrasting terms are business-to-consumer (B2C) and business-to-government (B2G). B2B branding is a term used in marketing.
Service	In economics, a service is an intangible commodity. That is, services are an example of intangible economic goods. Service provision is often an economic activity where the buyer does not generally, except by exclusive contract, obtain exclusive ownership of the thing purchased.

17. Managing Personal Communications: Direct and Database Marketing and Pe ...

CHAPTER HIGHLIGHTS & NOTES: KEY TERMS, PEOPLE, PLACES, CONCEPTS

Customer	A customer is the recipient of a good, service, product, or idea, obtained from a seller, vendor, or supplier for a monetary or other valuable consideration. Customers are generally categorized into two types:•An intermediate customer or trade customer who is a dealer that purchases goods for re-sale.•An ultimate customer who does not in turn re-sell the things bought but either passes them to the consumer or actually is the consumer. A customer may or may not also be a consumer, but the two notions are distinct, even though the terms are commonly confused. A customer purchases goods; a consumer uses them.
Database	A database is an organized collection of data. The data are typically organized to model aspects of reality in a way that supports processes requiring this information. For example, modelling the availability of rooms in hotels in a way that supports finding a hotel with vacancies.
Infomercial	An infomercial is a form of television commercial, which generally includes a phone number or website. Long-form infomercials are typically between 15 and (more commonly) 30 minutes in length. Sometimes shorter commercials are erroneously called infomercials (30 to 120 seconds in length with a call-to-action).
Home shopping	Home shopping is the electronic retailing and home shopping channels industry, which includes such billion dollar television-based and e-commerce companies as Liquidation Channel, HSN, QVC, eBay, ShopHQ, Buy.com, and Amazon.com, as well as traditional mail order and brick and mortar retailers as Hammacher Schlemmer and Sears, Roebuck and Co. Home shopping allows consumers to shop for goods from the privacy of their own home, as opposed to traditional shopping, which requires one to visit brick and mortar stores and shopping malls. There are three main types of home shopping: mail or telephone ordering from catalogs; telephone ordering in response to advertisements in print and electronic media (such as periodicals, TV and radio); and online shopping.
Marketing	Marketing is the process of communicating the value of a product or service to customers, for the purpose of selling that product or service. Marketing can be looked at as an organizational function and a set of processes for creating, delivering and communicating value to customers, and customer relationship management that also benefits the organization. Marketing is the science of choosing target markets through market analysis and market segmentation, as well as understanding consumer behavior and providing superior customer value.
Sales	A sale is the act of selling a product or service in return for money or other compensation. Signalling completion of the prospective stage, it is the beginning of an engagement between customer and vendor or the extension of that engagement.

17. Managing Personal Communications: Direct and Database Marketing and Pe ...

CHAPTER HIGHLIGHTS & NOTES: KEY TERMS, PEOPLE, PLACES, CONCEPTS

Relationship marketing	Relationship marketing was first defined as a form of marketing developed from direct response marketing campaigns which emphasizes customer retention and satisfaction, rather than a dominant focus on sales transactions. As a practice, relationship marketing differs from other forms of marketing in that it recognizes the long term value of customer relationships and extends communication beyond intrusive advertising and sales promotional messages. With the growth of the internet and mobile platforms, relationship marketing has continued to evolve and move forward as technology opens more collaborative and social communication channels.
Sales process	A sales process is an approach to selling a product or service. The sales process has been approached from the point of view of an engineering discipline .
Marketing management	Marketing management is a business discipline which focuses on the practical application of marketing techniques and the management of a firm's marketing resources and activities. Globalization has led firms to market beyond the borders of their home countries, making international marketing highly significant and an integral part of a firm's marketing strategy. Marketing managers are often responsible for influencing the level, timing, and composition of customer demand accepted definition of the term.
Account manager	An account manager is a person who works for a company and is responsible for the management of sales, and relationships with particular customers. The account manager does not manage the daily running of the account itself. They manage the relationship with the client of the account(s) they are assigned to.
Social marketing	Social marketing seeks to develop and integrate marketing concepts with other approaches to influence behaviors that benefit individuals and communities for the greater social good. It seeks to integrate research, best practice, theory, audience and partnership insight, to inform the delivery of competition sensitive and segmented social change programs that are effective, efficient, equitable and sustainable. Although 'social marketing' is sometimes seen only as using standard commercial marketing practices to achieve non-commercial goals, this is an oversimplification.
Social network	A social network is a social structure made up of a set of social actors and a set of the dyadic ties between these actors. The social network perspective provides a set of methods for analyzing the structure of whole social entities as well as a variety of theories explaining the patterns observed in these structures. The study of these structures uses social network analysis to identify local and global patterns, locate influential entities, and examine network dynamics.

17. Managing Personal Communications: Direct and Database Marketing and Pe ...

CHAPTER HIGHLIGHTS & NOTES: KEY TERMS, PEOPLE, PLACES, CONCEPTS

Selling	Selling is offering to exchange an item of value for a different item. The original item of value being offered may be either tangible or intangible. The second item, usually money, is most often seen by the seller as being of equal or greater value than that being offered for sale.
Feedback	Feedback is a process in which information about the past or the present influences the same phenomenon in the present or future. As part of a chain of cause-and-effect that forms a circuit or loop, the event is said to 'feed back' into itself. Feedback is also a synonym for:•Feedback signal - the measurement of the actual level of the parameter of interest.•Feedback mechanism - the action or means used to subsequently modify the gap.•Feedback loop - the complete causal path that leads from the initial detection of the gap to the subsequent modification of the gap.
Performance	A performance, in performing arts, generally comprises an event in which a performer or group of performers behave in a particular way for another group of people, the audience. Choral music and ballet are examples. Usually the performers participate in rehearsals beforehand.

CHAPTER QUIZ: KEY TERMS, PEOPLE, PLACES, CONCEPTS

1. A _____ is a collection of names and addresses used by an individual or an organization to send material to multiple recipients. The term is often extended to include the people subscribed to such a list, so the group of subscribers is referred to as 'the _____', or simply 'the list'.

    a. Mailing list
    b. Boardroom, Inc.
    c. Boiler room
    d. Book of the Month Club

2. . _____ is a form of direct marketing using databases of customers or potential customers to generate personalized communications in order to promote a product or service for marketing purposes. The method of communication can be any addressable medium, as in direct marketing.

    The distinction between direct and _____ stems primarily from the attention paid to the analysis of data.

    a. Berlin promotion agency
    b. Database marketing
    c. Boiler room

17. Managing Personal Communications: Direct and Database Marketing and Pe ...

CHAPTER QUIZ: KEY TERMS, PEOPLE, PLACES, CONCEPTS

3. A _____ is an approach to selling a product or service. The _____ has been approached from the point of view of an engineering discipline .

   a. Bill of sale
   b. Sales process
   c. Commission
   d. Conditional sale

4. An _____ is a person who works for a company and is responsible for the management of sales, and relationships with particular customers. The _____ does not manage the daily running of the account itself. They manage the relationship with the client of the account(s) they are assigned to.

   a. Army Club
   b. Account manager
   c. Bass diffusion model
   d. Bayesian inference in marketing

5. The _____ is intended to give U.S. consumers an opportunity to limit the telemarketing calls they receive. To register by telephone (US), consumers may call 1-888-382-1222; or they may register via the web at the DoNotCall.gov registration page. The registry was set to begin in 2003, but a court challenge delayed its implementation until 2004. The law provides exceptions to a blanket do-not-call ruling.

   a. Buw Holding
   b. National Do Not Call Registry
   c. Customer proprietary network information
   d. DialAmerica

ANSWER KEY
17. Managing Personal Communications: Direct and Database Marketing and Pe ...

1. a
2. b
3. b
4. b
5. b

You can take the complete Chapter Practice Test

for 17. Managing Personal Communications: Direct and Database Marketing and Pe ...

on all key terms, persons, places, and concepts.

Online 99 Cents

http://www.JustTheFacts101.com

Use www.JustTheFacts101.com for all your study needs

including Facts101's online interactive problem solving labs in

chemistry, statistics, mathematics, and more.

18. Managing Marketing Responsibly in the Global Economy

CHAPTER OUTLINE: KEY TERMS, PEOPLE, PLACES, CONCEPTS

- Globalization
- Service
- English auction
- Backward invention
- Distribution
- Marketing
- Marketing dashboard
- Cause-related marketing
- Greenwashing
- Social marketing
- Triple bottom line
- Customer
- Model

18. Managing Marketing Responsibly in the Global Economy

CHAPTER HIGHLIGHTS & NOTES: KEY TERMS, PEOPLE, PLACES, CONCEPTS

Globalization	Globalization is the process of international integration arising from the interchange of world views, products, ideas, and other aspects of culture. Advances in transportation and telecommunications infrastructure, including the rise of the telegraph and its posterity the Internet, are major factors in globalization, generating further interdependence of economic and cultural activities. Though scholars place the origins of globalization in modern times, others trace its history long before the European age of discovery and voyages to the New World.
Service	In economics, a service is an intangible commodity. That is, services are an example of intangible economic goods. Service provision is often an economic activity where the buyer does not generally, except by exclusive contract, obtain exclusive ownership of the thing purchased.
English auction	An English auction is a type of auction, whose most typical form is the 'open outcry' auction. The auctioneer opens the auction by announcing a Suggested Opening Bid, a starting price or reserve for the item on sale and then accepts increasingly higher bids from the floor consisting of buyers with a possible interest in the item. Unlike sealed bid auctions, 'open outcry' auctions are 'open' or fully transparent as the identity of all bidders is disclosed to each other during the auction.
Backward invention	Backward invention is a product strategy in international marketing in which an existing product may have to be re-engineered or dumbed down by the company to be released in less developed countries, often at a cheaper rate. Doing so can often breathe new life into an obsolete product by the company or even target people too poor to afford the actual product.
Distribution	Product distribution is one of the four elements of the marketing mix. Distribution is the process of making a product or service available for use or consumption by a consumer or business user, using direct means, or using indirect means with intermediaries. The other three parts of the marketing mix are product, pricing, and promotion.
Marketing	Marketing is the process of communicating the value of a product or service to customers, for the purpose of selling that product or service. Marketing can be looked at as an organizational function and a set of processes for creating, delivering and communicating value to customers, and customer relationship management that also benefits the organization. Marketing is the science of choosing target markets through market analysis and market segmentation, as well as understanding consumer behavior and providing superior customer value.

18. Managing Marketing Responsibly in the Global Economy

CHAPTER HIGHLIGHTS & NOTES: KEY TERMS, PEOPLE, PLACES, CONCEPTS

Marketing dashboard	Marketing performance measurement and management is a term used by marketing professionals to describe the analysis and improvement of the efficiency and effectiveness of marketing. This is accomplished by focus on the alignment of marketing activities, strategies, and metrics with business goals. It involves the creation of a metrics framework to monitor marketing performance, and then develop and utilize marketing dashboards to manage marketing performance.
Cause-related marketing	Cause marketing or cause-related marketing refers to a type of marketing involving the cooperative efforts of a for profit business and a non-profit organization for mutual benefit. The term is sometimes used more broadly and generally to refer to any type of marketing effort for social and other charitable causes, including in-house marketing efforts by non-profit organizations. Cause marketing differs from corporate giving (philanthropy), as the latter generally involves a specific donation that is tax deductible, while cause marketing is a marketing relationship not necessarily based on a donation.
Greenwashing	Greenwashing, or 'green sheen,' is a form of spin in which green PR or green marketing is deceptively used to promote the perception that an organization's products, aims or policies are environmentally friendly. Evidence that an organization is greenwashing often comes from pointing out the spending differences: when significantly more money or time has been spent advertising being 'green' (that is, operating with consideration for the environment), than is actually spent on environmentally sound practices. Greenwashing efforts can range from changing the name or label of a product to evoke the natural environment on a product that contains harmful chemicals to multimillion dollar advertising campaigns portraying highly polluting energy companies as eco-friendly.
Social marketing	Social marketing seeks to develop and integrate marketing concepts with other approaches to influence behaviors that benefit individuals and communities for the greater social good. It seeks to integrate research, best practice, theory, audience and partnership insight, to inform the delivery of competition sensitive and segmented social change programs that are effective, efficient, equitable and sustainable. Although 'social marketing' is sometimes seen only as using standard commercial marketing practices to achieve non-commercial goals, this is an oversimplification.
Triple bottom line	Triple bottom line is an accounting framework with three parts: social, environmental (or ecological) and financial. These three divisions are also called the three Ps: people, planet and profit, or the 'three pillars of sustainability'. Interest in triple bottom line accounting has been growing in both for-profit, nonprofit and government sectors.
Customer	A customer is the recipient of a good, service, product, or idea, obtained from a seller, vendor, or supplier for a monetary or other valuable consideration.

18. Managing Marketing Responsibly in the Global Economy

CHAPTER HIGHLIGHTS & NOTES: KEY TERMS, PEOPLE, PLACES, CONCEPTS

Customers are generally categorized into two types:•An intermediate customer or trade customer who is a dealer that purchases goods for re-sale.•An ultimate customer who does not in turn re-sell the things bought but either passes them to the consumer or actually is the consumer.

A customer may or may not also be a consumer, but the two notions are distinct, even though the terms are commonly confused. A customer purchases goods; a consumer uses them.

Model

A model, is a person in a role either to promote, display, or advertise commercial products (notably fashion clothing) or to serve as a visual aide for people who are creating works of art.

Modelling ('modeling' in American English) is considered to be different from other types of public performance, such as an acting, dancing or being a mime artist. The boundary between modelling and performing is, however, not well defined, although such activities as appearing in a movie or a play are almost never labelled as modelling.

CHAPTER QUIZ: KEY TERMS, PEOPLE, PLACES, CONCEPTS

1. Product _____ is one of the four elements of the marketing mix. _____ is the process of making a product or service available for use or consumption by a consumer or business user, using direct means, or using indirect means with intermediaries.

   The other three parts of the marketing mix are product, pricing, and promotion.

   a. Back to school
   b. Backward invention
   c. Distribution
   d. Bayesian inference in marketing

2. In economics, a _____ is an intangible commodity. That is, _____s are an example of intangible economic goods.

   _____ provision is often an economic activity where the buyer does not generally, except by exclusive contract, obtain exclusive ownership of the thing purchased.

   a. Bad
   b. Cargo
   c. Service
   d. Club good

18. Managing Marketing Responsibly in the Global Economy

CHAPTER QUIZ: KEY TERMS, PEOPLE, PLACES, CONCEPTS

3. _____ is the process of international integration arising from the interchange of world views, products, ideas, and other aspects of culture. Advances in transportation and telecommunications infrastructure, including the rise of the telegraph and its posterity the Internet, are major factors in _____, generating further interdependence of economic and cultural activities.

   Though scholars place the origins of _____ in modern times, others trace its history long before the European age of discovery and voyages to the New World.

   a. Tulip mania
   b. Millenary Petition
   c. Globalization
   d. Yasukuni

4. A _____, is a person in a role either to promote, display, or advertise commercial products (notably fashion clothing) or to serve as a visual aide for people who are creating works of art.

   Modelling ('modeling' in American English) is considered to be different from other types of public performance, such as an acting, dancing or being a mime artist. The boundary between modelling and performing is, however, not well defined, although such activities as appearing in a movie or a play are almost never labelled as modelling.

   a. Billboard
   b. Bibliography of advertising
   c. Bespoke Music
   d. Model

5. An _____ is a type of auction, whose most typical form is the 'open outcry' auction. The auctioneer opens the auction by announcing a Suggested Opening Bid, a starting price or reserve for the item on sale and then accepts increasingly higher bids from the floor consisting of buyers with a possible interest in the item. Unlike sealed bid auctions, 'open outcry' auctions are 'open' or fully transparent as the identity of all bidders is disclosed to each other during the auction.

   a. Bid shading
   b. English auction
   c. Bidding fee auction
   d. Bid-to-cover ratio

ANSWER KEY
18. Managing Marketing Responsibly in the Global Economy

1. c
2. c
3. c
4. d
5. b

You can take the complete Chapter Practice Test

for 18. Managing Marketing Responsibly in the Global Economy
on all key terms, persons, places, and concepts.

Online 99 Cents

http://www.JustTheFacts101.com

Use www.JustTheFacts101.com for all your study needs including Facts101's online interactive problem solving labs in chemistry, statistics, mathematics, and more.

Other Facts101 e-Books and Tests

Want More?
JustTheFacts101.com...

Jtf101.com provides the outlines and highlights of your textbooks, just like this e-StudyGuide, but also gives you the PRACTICE TESTS, and other exclusive study tools for all of your textbooks.

Learn More. *Just click*
http://www.JustTheFacts101.com/